No More
Next Time

Marketing in the Age of
Distraction

John Oxford

No More Next Time – Marketing in the Age of Distraction
Published by Oxford Productions, LLC

Inquiries for speaking requests or information should be addressed to:
John Oxford
209 Troy Street
Tupelo, MS 38804

Text: **662-205-6288**
Email: **campaignmarketinghelp@gmail.com**.

www.johnoxford.com
www.marketingmoneypodcast.com

Cover design: Corey Childers
Editing and interior design: Chris O'Byrne
Writing support: Kristen White

Printed in the United States of America

ISBN: 978-1-64184-299-0 (paperback)
ISBN: 978-1-64184-300-3 (ebook)

This book is dedicated to the 2 that takes care of the 3.

CONTENTS

INTRODUCTION

You might look at this book and think, *I've already seen a thousand marketing books; why does there need to be one more?* The reason I wrote this book is that there are too many marketing mistakes still happening in the marketplace. A lot of marketing is based on old, traditional marketing that doesn't work with today's new tactics. I still see a lot of people who don't pay for quality production, a lot of people who don't place a video properly, and a lot of people who don't seem to have a plan that can convert off their content. I thought it was time to take my expertise and write a book about how you can put everything together simply for a better marketing experience for you and your customer.

With more than twenty years of experience with marketing, politics, academia—and a little bit of music, I believe I have a good blend of experience for a marketer. My first job was at age seventeen as a taste-tester for Nabisco. They interviewed me for the job, and because I was a teen with an opinion, they chose me out of a large group, along with four or five other kids, to taste test some of their new food. After you tasted it, you would rate it, and then watch a video or a commercial about what you just ate, and rate if that looked like or felt like the food. The ones you chose would end up being rated, and then you might see them on TV.

Although it was a great job, there were only so many Nutter Butters, peanut butter sandwiches, and Oreos I could eat. I decided not to be like an NBA athlete, skip college, and become a professional taste-tester. I decided to go to college instead. But that experience was how I got started in marketing.

I went to the University of Tennessee, then went into a management trainee program for First Union bank out of Charlotte, NC. I then left banking for about five years which included working for the George W. Bush administration.

I was in a communication positions in Health and Human Services, as well as the Office of Management and Budget. It was a fun job for a junior staffer, as far as political appointee jobs go, until 9/11 happened. Like everyone else, my world was changed. I was part of the group that helped prepare the legislation for the Department of Homeland Security that was started shortly after 9/11. (When I say I was part of it, I mean I was nothing more than a note-taker—but I learned a great deal from this experience.)

I worked for three years in Washington and then decided DC had gotten a little hectic. I also wanted to move back to the South. I met my wife and then moved to Mississippi, where I took a job at the University of Mississippi (Ole Miss) as a communication instructor. After teaching for a year and a half, which was one of the greatest experiences of my life, it was time to get back into the corporate world.

My wife was working at the Ole Miss as well. As luck would have it, I taught my bank's CEO's son, who was also conveniently from my wife's hometown of Tupelo, Mississippi, which is still a very tight-knit community. After a few interviews, I joined Renasant Bank, which is where I am today. I've now been there for fifteen years, and we've gone from $2.7 billion in assets to approximately $13.4 billion during my time with the company.

In addition, I'm an instructor with the Stonier Executive Bank Management School for the American Bankers Association, which is taught at the Wharton Business School at the University of Pennsylvania, the Mississippi Bankers School of Banking at Ole Miss, and the Graduate School of Banking Staff at LSU. I think that all those experiences make for a nice combo to write a book about my experiences, where I think marketing should go, and what the new fundamentals should be in 2020.

In today's marketplace, there are too many obvious mistakes. One is too much sameness. For example, if a dentist does an ad, the next dentist wants to do that same ad. Car dealership advertisements, especially on a local level, are all the same with somebody shouting, "We have the best deal; no one beats our deal!" There's a sea of sameness out there, and I think it comes from fear, a lack of creativity, a lack of content direction, and also lack of professional and sophisticated messaging.

All businesses want to be efficient, but many are either too cheap to hire agencies or experts or hire low-cost but ineffective people. Many think TV advertising is the way to go, and others still think print advertisement is where their ad dollars should be. There is a place for all this in your marketing mix, but consumption has rapidly changed.

You can control many of your own channels now. You can control your medium, and you can build your own audiences. It's not just for big television stations as it was in the 1980s. Today you now have many channels to reach almost everyone. And we're not even talking about cable television channels; we're also talking about social media and all of the new platforms available to everyone. Moving away from the cheapness of cutting corners in production for advertising all the way up to the macro level of marketing, the question is where to get the best bang for your buck and what are the steps you need to take to get there?

The title, *No More Next Time*, came about because, in today's world, experience and time are more important than ever. If you miss the chance to provide an amazing or expected customer experience, whether it be through content, connection, or conversion, if you miss a chance, there is no more next time. It's a cliché example, but Amazon has taken over the ability to sell things with a click. You can also get into your hotel room, skipping the front desk, using your phone as a digital key. You can shop for shoes on Facebook and have them instantly delivered the next day. Knowing that, there's really no more next time if you miss your chance with your customer.

Marketers have to realize that the conversion process is just as important as the content and the connection. You might have the best content, and you may have the most connective messaging, but if you can't convert a customer, you've lost your opportunity. There is no more next time in today's world because it's so fast, moving with the click of a button. Let me repeat, if you don't know how to convert or know how to catch your client, you've missed your opportunity.

The subtitle for this book, *Marketing in the Age of Distraction*, is because we are all very distracted. We're doing too many things at the same time. How do you cut through the distraction? I think that great content that connects with an audience WILL cut through the distraction. You have to steal interest from those with whom you compete. If you're a bank, you're not just competing with other banks. You're competing with Budweiser, Nike, and Toyota. If you're Toyota, you're not just competing with Ford, Chevy, and Nissan, you're competing with Budweiser, watch companies, phone companies, and whomever else is producing content. It's the distraction of the entire market, not just your industry. In addition, whatever is on TV is losing to the distraction of mobile devices.

Marketing is much more holistic now. It used to be that you bought television ads or you bought print ads. Now, who even reads the newspaper? Some people still do, but how are you reaching your audience? You must have a holistic look at your marketing because, if you just do print, TV, or direct mail, you're missing out on the vast reach of social media. If you're just doing social media, you're missing out on digital advertising along with SEO and SEM opportunities. Digital advertising includes social media, but it also includes things like geo-fencing, native advertisement, organic placement, web, etc.

If you have all of these things that come in digital as well as traditional, how are you testing it? Are you making changes from your test to then deploy your marketing, and what adjustments are you making to be more successful? And the most important thing is: how are you converting these clients once you get their attention?

Many people have asked me why I would write a book now when I'm in the middle of a great job with a growing family, three active kids, and three kinds of teacherships. I'm busy—very busy. But when I attend or speak at conferences, I wonder why the hired speakers—often former CMOs—didn't write a book like this while they were still working in the jungle of marketing versus reflecting after they got out of it. I wondered why not have someone who's actually in the mix right now put together what's going on and what they're seeing versus maybe being three or four years out of the field.

Marketing is changing very fast. It is probably the most rapid thing that changes in business. Releasing a new product, for example, has to be made, tested, and regulated. Marketing can be a video on your phone shot last night where you're talking. It's so fast and so rapid, and yet it has to have the tactics gleaned from a foundation, but also has to be looked at analytically. Can you analyze what's going on and then test it, make adjustments, and put it in the marketplace? It changes so rapidly that if you wait three or four months (not years!), some things you're talking about may not even exist anymore. It's very important in marketing to be in the now, and I think you have to know that with social media apps changing every day, the conversion process is changing every day as well.

Are you paying with Apple Pay and Google Pay? Are you paying with cash? How are you converting a client? The marketing of that process can change every single day. Being up to speed on it, being in the now and in the know creates a good foundation for you, but it also creates the ability for you to be successful as a marketer.

Let's look at strategy versus tactics. A lot of books are all about ideas, and they go into stories and deep dives about strategy, but then they never get into how you tactically execute what you're reading. The most hackneyed example is Nike. Every marketer loves talking about "Just Do It" and Nike. But what does that do for Jim's auto body shop down the street or the community bank on the corner?

Not a whole lot. Jim's auto body shop doesn't want to know about Nike. They want to know how they can promote their business. The strategy of a major company might not work for your local business, and your local business strategy may not work for the big national or global company. This book sets a new principle foundation to cut through the big strategy as well as proven tactics.

In this book, we'll discuss slogans. We'll talk about social media, digital placement, content writing, as well as copywriting. These are just some of the takeaways. We also look into the differences between strategy and tactics. *Strategy* is planning the way you want something to happen. *Tactics* are what you do to execute your strategy. So you've got to set a strategy first.

What is our strategy? To open accounts and get clients to know our brand? And what's the tactic(s) to get there? Is it social, digital, television, print, billboards, and/or radio? What is it that gets you there? The *how* and *why* is the strategy. The *getting there* is the tactic.

So what are the four Cs and the four Ps?

The four Ps are considered the traditional foundation of marketing in the '50s by Professor Neil Borden, who taught marketing at Harvard. He laid down the groundwork that is typically recognized as the foundation of marketing: place, product, promotion, and price.

Old Marketing	New Marketing
Price	Content
Placement	Connection
Product	Conversion
Promotion	Campaigns

However, marketing has changed a lot since the '50s and '60s, and it's time to change the Ps to the four Cs: content, connection, conversion, and campaigns. The four Cs are more relevant in today's marketplace than the four Ps. We're going to modernize the four Ps into the four Cs, and that's the baseline for the chapters in this book.

Neil Borden taught the four Ps as part of *The Concept of the Marketing Mix*, which was a book written in 1964. He and Jerome McCarthy, who is a professor at Michigan State, also wrote a book called *Basic Marketing—A Managerial Approach*. Now, a managerial approach may sound very boring, but every MBA 101 class teaches the four Ps. I would argue that the four Ps have changed. Promotion is just one part of marketing and is very different from how it was done in the '50s and '60s, which was television, newspaper, radio or door-to-door sales. It was promoting the *product*.

Now it's so vastly different that promotion falls into *connection*. How are you communicating and connecting? How are you connecting with your promotion? Does product matter as much as it used to? Because it's rapidly changing. Is product a part of marketing? I don't know that it is. It's what you're selling. The product could be you. Product makes me think of something physical. With today's world marketing, you might not even be marketing a physical product. It's an experience. It's what your client needs.

Now comes the content side of it. And then you talk about a place as one of the Ps. Place is irrelevant now, especially with the Internet. In the 1950s, people thought there had to be a place that they had to go down to Sears and Roebuck and buy their clothing, or they had to go to the shoe store to get shoes, etc.

With the click of a button, things just show up at your front door. When I deal with local businesses, I remind them that when they say we don't need a website. We don't need to be active on Facebook. I say, "**There's nothing more local than your front door.**" And so when they argue that they're the local business and Amazon's not, Amazon is delivering to that client's front door. There is nothing more local than your front door!

Small businesses and local companies must realize and take advantage of the digital world is out there. They have to take advantage of it just as much as the big guys, which levels the playing field for all. When we talk about *place*, it doesn't really seem relevant because there doesn't have to be a physical place anymore. It's how it gets there and how it converts. So we're going to replace the four Ps with the four Cs, and that's going to be the base of this book.

Price has also evolved because now there are resellers in the marketplace. Companies like eBay have created a resale market. Price is something that can't be controlled like it used to be in the past. When the four Ps were created, the idea was a company comes up with a *product*, they *price* it, they put it in a *place*, and they *promote* it. **Really simple.**

Today, it's not so simple since the price can change through other delivery methods. There are resellers, wholesalers, and websites that can get things at a different price from somewhere else. Sourcing is different today. Of course, the place is different because of the Internet, so pricing changes, placements change, and products change every day. Promotion is totally different from what it used to be.

The four Ps have completely changed so much that we're turning them into the four Cs for an update to a foundational marketing book. Hopefully, when people read this, they think about marketing from the perspective of the four Cs.

It's worth mentioning there's a fifth hidden P that's not talked about as much: *people*. People, which becomes a part of communication, are still important in marketing, especially since we've gone so digital. The consumer is still a person who has to click to purchase the product. It's really about how you connect to your audience. You've got to connect to people through your content and then convert them through campaigns. People are very, very important, duh. You've got to be aware of people and how you connect to them. That's what makes marketing successful, even in today's digital delivery of marketing.

We have more distractions now than ever before. How do you cut through those distractions? It starts with really, really good content. What grabs a person? It could be silly videos or gut-wrenching, tear-jerking videos. Create content that catches and cuts through the distraction.

A lot of marketers are afraid to do it because it's a risk. When you get attention, you cut through the distraction, and that's what really good marketing is all about in today's world. You can throw a lot of money behind marketing, which big companies often do, where the content doesn't have to be as great. Then someone can come along with a good idea that's somewhat original and create great content with a great delivery, and they can interrupt the distraction and grab attention. Many companies and industries do it well, and we discuss some of those in this book.

Five seconds. That's all you have to capture a consumer's attention. In public speaking, experts say the first 30 seconds are the most important because people form their opinion of you quickly. The first 30 seconds is how you walk out on stage, what you're wearing, how you look, how you talk—and the judging starts. Are your hands shaking? Are you nervous? People are judging and forming opinions. It's even faster in the digital marketplace. If the music doesn't connect, if the person doesn't look like you, feel like you, or relate to you, you're clicking off, scrolling up, or swiping to move on. If the ad on television doesn't catch your attention, you're picking up your phone and looking at other content. It's got to catch your attention immediately. You have about a five-second window to cut through distraction, and that's why properly produced content is so important.

> **Five seconds. That's all the time you have to capture the consumer's attention.**

There's no next time, and here's a good example. A few years ago, I was in the market for some new golf clubs. I went to a local pro I knew and told him I wanted to invest in some new clubs. We looked through a few sets, and I tried about seven or eight different types before I found the exact kind I wanted to order.

He said they were out of stock, so I couldn't get those clubs. I pointed out that someone should be able to get them, whether it be from eBay, Amazon, Dick's Sporting Goods, etc. There's got to be a way to find these golf clubs! Unfortunately, he couldn't get them for me. I won't say it was laziness, but I will say it was a lack of expertise in the digital marketplace.

I went online, found the exact clubs I wanted and had them delivered. A little while later, I was on the golf course with a buddy, and he said, "Hey, the pro was upset because you didn't buy your golf clubs from him."

I said, "He couldn't get the ones I wanted."

And he said, "Well, that guy made a mistake because he should've just gone online and bought them, then just up-charged and sold them to you. You'd never have known the difference."

There was no more next time because of the availability of technology.

That's an example of the marketplace today; if someone tells you they can't get something, you may still be able to (although often at a price). Take concerts, for example. Nobody can say they can't get a ticket just because they are sold out on Ticketmaster. They'll likely have to pay more, but they can still get that ticket. The disruption in the marketplace of "no more next time" is because someone else can sell it to you or find it. Depending on what you're willing to pay, you can get just about anything.

The golf pro could've gone online for the golf clubs, marked them up, sold them to me, and he would've gotten a win. I would've gotten a win. There is no next time when you don't understand the digital means—the secondary market—in the ways people can receive things and how products are marketed and delivered today.

In today's marketplace, there are more opportunities to touch, reach, feel, attract, cut through to disruption, and get to your customer than ever before. The problem is that everyone's doing it or trying to do it. Some do it better than others, but in the '50s, you bought a television show. "This evening's show is brought to you by GE," or "This evening's show is brought to you by

Palmolive," or some other conglomerate business that would actually pay for the show. Hollywood would go sell the shows to marketing agencies, and they'd partner them up with a brand to sell.

The crazy thing is that the content concept still works today. You can find or make a show, sponsor and distribute it online. The shows could be as short as just a few minutes, promotional in nature, about the background of an athlete or rock star, or of a business and how things are made. The strategy of marketing in the 1950s is probably foundationally more relevant today in content than what happened in the '80s when it was just like a free-for-all. People bought all types of television, put ads everywhere, went to the four major networks and looked at Nielsen ratings, then just threw their ads out there and thought, *This is going to work!*

The winners were typically the ones who could buy the most television. Creativity was okay, but think about the '80s—do you remember a lot of the advertising being creative? Probably not. You just saw it a lot because people bought gross rating points by the thousands.

GROSS RATING POINTS

What are gross rating points?

According to MarketingProfs.com, Gross Rating Points (GRPs) are a standard measure in advertising. They measure advertising impact. It's calculated as a percent of the target market reached multiplied by the exposure frequency. Thus, if you get to advertise to 30% of the target market and give them four exposures, you will have 120 GRPs.

Just like most measures, you need to have an understanding of the reach and the limitations of GRPs. People like to think of them as a measure of impact, but that is really overstated. Impact should measure sales; this measures exposures (in fact, it's assumed exposures). So you need to be careful in thinking that 120 GRPs represent something tangible.

When people bought rating points, they would base their success on how many people saw something and how well the brand was recognized. Today is a little different. You can measure through digital means. With television, you can't click and buy. But online, you can click on the ad, and if it's done properly, you can get conversion points you can actually measure. Today, creativity and connection play a much deeper role in connecting to that customer and then getting them to convert—whether it be a click or actually visiting your place of business.

All of this ties into grabbing attention. How do you get the attention of the consumer to look at your brand versus someone else's brand? We're going to talk about content a lot because it's the first C, and you've got to own your content. There are many ways to do that; it shouldn't just start with a commercial. Don't look at content as a commercial; look at it as your brand message and the embodiment of who you are. You're not selling a product; you're selling a solution.

NAPSTER AND THE IPHONE

In the mid-2000s, everything changed. It started with something that most people probably wouldn't think was that big of a change, but it was—and it was Napster. Gen Xers remember Napster as the first public file-sharing network where you could steal—I mean "save"—music. It actually was stealing because people were stealing IP from someone else. They would share it with you, then you could put it on your computer and build a song catalog.

You could find people who liked the same music you did, and it was sort of the first time you could chat. Myspace was coming along, but Napster was really the first super public interactive file sharing, as well as chat organization, that everyone got into because, let's face it, music is universal and it was free. They saw it and thought, *Wow, I'll get on Napster, and I'm not paying for music. I've been spending all this money on CDs, records, and tapes,* and it was the first time music could be acquired digitally. And it was easy!

Of course, it wrecked the record industry, but it gave us the means and recognition of transferring data, and that created the highway. Napster created the pop culture thought of a highway of transferring information. Nowadays, that includes iTunes, Google Play, delivery channels such as Pandora and Spotify, Amazon music—all these ways of delivering music and movies. There's also YouTube, Netflix, Prime Video, Disney Plus, HBO Go, ESPN Go—many different ways of delivering content. If you think about it, it started with Napster. I know a lot of people may not want to process it that way because it probably gives Napster too much credit, but Napster was the first publicly and popularly accepted file sharing apparatus in the United States. Just ask Metallica.

Now, that's our highway. What's the vehicle that gets us there today? It's the iPhone, which came out in 2007, and the Android phone. In 2007, you now had something in your hand that could deliver content to you, and the world completely changed. File sharing and the intranet is a highway, and the car to get you there was that phone. Put those two together and all of a sudden you can deliver content to someone in a way that is personal and in their hand, they can click on it and have it delivered to their doorstep if it's a physical product, and if it's something like music, movies, or something that's not physical but an experiential product, it's delivered directly and immediately.

What is Mass Intimacy?

In the online Masterclass series with Jeff Goodby and Rich Silverstein of the GS&P Agency, the agency of got milk?, Bud-weis-er frogs to lizards, and Sam Elliott and Lil Nas X Dorito Super Bowl commercial fame, they speak of mass intimacy in modern marketing. It's the idea that we consume marketing content on our phone that is right in front of us, thus it's intimate and no longer in a room with a TV and other people. Your marketing must be made for mass intimacy or it will get lost in its connection to your audience.

Around 2000, everything changed because of file sharing apps and the apparatus of delivery. And then when phones became computers and in 2007, that gave us the vehicle to get us where we are today. You now have a method to deliver content.

How do you connect to people who are more concerned about pricing than those who just want an experience or the brand they trust?

With the rise of the mobile phone and the highway of getting content, social media was introduced. It provided a way for people to connect as they've never connected before, which, in some ways, is scary. Opinions, politics, brand, reviews, and looking at how everyone interacts with each other personalized brands. No longer was it just Popeyes Chicken, it was the chicken sandwich you're tweeting about and texting to your friends. It was a bad experience at a hotel or with a car, and you're telling everyone about it, so you're amplifying the communication from brands. It allowed people to connect better and changed lifestyles.

Instead of watching your favorite shows only on a television set, you're streaming and watching them on your phone anytime you want. Instead of being more physically social, you're digitally social now. What used to be getting together at a high school reunion is now a Facebook page for your high school class. I saw a great ad one time that said, "Update your Facebook profile in person; attend your high school reunion." There are many people who won't go to high school reunions anymore because they just see everybody on Facebook. I know what they're doing on Facebook. I know what they're doing on Instagram. I know what they're doing on Twitter.

The phone provided the ability to always be connected, which has changed us. It's made us more distracted because we can easily distract ourselves. You can step out of the real world and watch shows, a Facebook video, or connect with somebody via direct message or over LinkedIn. Distractions are so readily available that we're almost constantly distracted now. How do you cut through that? That's what you'll learn in the coming chapters.

Along with the change in social media, phones, the ability to file share, and transfer and connect, we can spend money digitally as well via apps like Zelle, PayPal, and Venmo. We also have to understand that the same old marketing doesn't work. Take billboards for example, while they're static and can have a memorable message, are not as memorable as they used to be because people are listening to satellite radio or on their phones – yes, even while driving. You can even go to a store, and rather than shop for a product, you might actually look at a price for something you can see and then buy online if it's less expensive. Thus, no more next time. If the store cannot "close" you while you're there shopping, they've missed their chance. They've missed their turn.

That's why marketing to the consumer in many different ways, in a holistic way, is so important, because if they're in the store, you have to get them while they're there. They might not even be shopping for your product but instead are shopping for how they can get a product somewhere else at a better price. You've got to be aware of these different avenues, and it cannot be expressed enough how important digital marketing and the digital experience to a customer is just as important today as an in-store experience or a personal experience.

With all of these changes in shopping behavior, human interaction has changed. Traffic count used to be a big deal. There's a billboard on the corner "seen" by 5,000 cars a day, but do they really see it? Does the traffic count matter anymore? I work for a financial services institution that lets you deposit your check over the phone. That has the potential to take a lot of people out of the branch. What's going to be the most important job in a bank in the next few years? Probably digital password resetting and coding for security or online protection of all those online accounts versus opening an account, which you can do online as well. It won't be cashing a check anymore.

But that's a bigger picture of how things have changed a lot with interaction. It might also be how many views are you getting? How many impressions are you getting? How many clicks are you getting? Those Key Performance Indicators (KPIs) may be more important than just the traffic count you're getting with cars into your restaurant, or what you're getting with your website, because those important points, those things you need to know, change so rapidly. A restaurant partnering with Uber Eats may deliver more food than what they sell to people sitting at the tables in their restaurant, and that can change the whole dynamic of their business. It might be how fast they can get quality food out versus a great server delivering an experience to that customer.

The marketplace is changing rapidly, and how you adapt to it with content, connection, and then convert those clients through campaigns is why this book was written. As you go through this book, you'll learn about the four Cs and their replacement of the four Ps. These four Cs will set up your battle plan to be a successful brand marketer. Your plan will be delivered through content, which pulls in the connection. How do you connect with your consumers? How do you cut through the distraction? We don't just do it to make pretty pictures or funny stories or interesting concepts, we actually have to convert because business is about making money. There *is* a bottom line.

Publicly traded companies have to report earnings. If you're in sales, you have to report your sales numbers. We must ask the question: How do we convert off this great content that connects and creates beautiful marketing? How does it convert digitally, physically, or however you get to your customer? Finally, using these in a campaign? Let's go through examples of different campaigns where content was used well to connect to a client and convert to close the sale. We'll also look at some that didn't go so well.

In today's marketplace, where there's more distraction than ever, the four Cs to make you a successful brander are: content, connection, conversion, and campaign. If you master the four Cs, you will be successful, your business will be successful, and you will do well as a marketer.

CHAPTER 1
THE FIRST C: CONTENT

"There is no such thing as a new idea. It is impossible. We simply take a lot of old ideas and put them into a sort of mental kaleidoscope. We give them a turn and they make new and curious combinations. We keep on turning and making new combinations indefinitely; but they are the same old pieces of colored glass that have been in use through all the ages."

–Mark Twain

All modern marketing starts with content because it's the delivery of information. Content is information delivered to an audience. Content marketing is taking that information and making it something engaging that leads to a sale. GS&P describe marketing as art serving commerce. It's really pretty simple: content is information, and content marketing is taking that information with a purpose to sell to an audience. When Mark Twain, or Samuel Clemmons, said there are no original ideas, which meant there was nothing new. I think that's a lot of the holdup in marketing. Look back at successful branders like Elvis Presley. He borrowed a lot of his style and look from the comic book character Captain Marvel Jr and was influenced in many ways by the black community of Shake Rag in Tupelo, Mississippi. There's a misnomer that content has to be something new. Marketers beat their heads against the wall, thinking they've got to have a new, great idea.

My father, who was a marketer himself, used to say, "It either has to be different or the best to stand out." And if it's both of those, you win. Otherwise, you're just part of the mushy middle area, the boring average. With content, you have the chance to set yourself apart with something that makes you different or makes you the best. You can do that by finding your brand, which starts with content because that's information you're delivering to the marketplace. What is your content, and what should it be? It all depends on what you're selling or what your product is, but it's important to know that the information you deliver becomes your brand. That's why all marketing starts with content.

Content is many things. You may think of content as a video on your phone, but content is like branding. It's everything around your business or brand message. It can be anything from your slogan to your tagline—even your name or your logo. It's all the parts of your content that builds the brand. Marketing always starts with content because your content is information about who you are, and content marketing is the delivery of that information.

It's important that you hit every aspect of content with a fine-toothed comb. As you're looking over your brand, is it the kerning of the letters in your logo and in the words of your brand? Is it the name of your brand? Is it your tagline? Is it the way it's delivered to your audience? What's your brand message? What are the feelings it gives? Is it high value, a brand that someone will pay more to receive? Is it low value where the person knows that they're getting it on the cheap, but it's what they want? All that is part of content and the way it's delivered in the messaging of your content marketing.

Looking at content is a two-way street. Your consumers can send content back to you, whether it be reviews or videos or research, which helps you adjust your marketing and your strategy because the consumer will often spot what's wrong before the company will. A great example of this is the bow tie story.

How many men know how to tie a bow tie? I don't know what the percentage is, but if you're in a wedding or have to go to a formal event, you might struggle to figure out how to tie a bow tie at the last second. Well, YouTube has solved that problem. There is a company in Ohio that sold bow ties. They had one of their haberdashers go online and do a video of him tying one, and at the time of this writing, it's had over six million views on YouTube: https://www.youtube.com/watch?v=5X4aBSRt_HQ. That video is content. And guess what? People now shop online with that company for bow ties. They sell hundreds of bow ties over the Internet because of a video of one of their guys tying a bow tie.

That is a great example of good yet simple content for something that solves a problem. They did not sell a product. They solved a problem by showing how to tie a bow tie, and it created a marketplace for them on the Internet. It worked completely through content and content delivery. That's how consumers want to feel the content from their brands now. It's not an interruptive commercial on television, it's "here's what you can do with it," messaging. It's like Lowes and Home Depot telling you how to do it yourself with content on remodeling your home.

"Be the show, not the commercial."

–David BeeBe

Content being a two-way street also has to be set up to meet a customer's expectations. If they Google "how to fix an ice maker," you can search and figure out how to do that yourself or pay someone to do it because there are different markets for this. You can search how to tie a bow tie, and companies literally put the answers on the Internet with video or with blogs, or any way that meets the customer's demand for content. Again, good content is a two-way street. It meets the demand of the consumer and also delivers a brand message and solution to a continuous problem. That's what makes content so vastly important today because you're receiving content on your brand and adjusting to it and delivering what the customer needs.

Content has changed tremendously over the last few decades. It used to only be that you'd see something on TV or read it in the paper. You'd consider buying it and doing so when the time was right. You saw an ad for Dove soap, and you thought, *Hey, I need some soap!* You like to be clean, and so you're going to go buy some soap. Dove had made a commercial, and so you had brand awareness of Dove, so you went to the store and bought the soap you wanted.

In today's world, the consumer sitting on their couch with their phone can just Google the best soap brands. They will get a long list of websites that will deliver different types of soap. They'll click, and then have it delivered right to their house.

Content for the delivery might be actually more important for selling the experience of why your soap is better than others, and getting the content on your site versus just putting an ad on television or the newspaper goes a long way. Bank marketing, for example, is where consumers often believe all banks are the same. Consumers often go to the bank down the street or the location closest to them. Now, you can search for banks online and find various types of checking accounts, digitally sign up for one, and be on your way without actually having gone to the bank.

Content has to be made to reach out to the customer as the customer is looking for what they want, and if you're not prepared to answer their questions, there is no next time because they're ready to make that decision right then and there. There won't be a next time if your content isn't ready. When they're ready to make the decision, it's on their terms and not yours anymore.

Hours of business no longer exist because the consumer can get what they want anytime they want it, especially when delivered via digital means. Content has to meet the consumer where they want to be met, whether it's a video explaining how to fix something, or how to write a book. You can find all this stuff out on the Internet. Now you have to execute it. That's where you win—not with what you want the consumer to see, but what the consumer wants to see and find from you.

When you're building your content, look at the production quality. If the production is not good, it may represent the product as not being good. A lot of people miss out on today's modern marketing thinking they can get an iPhone, shoot a commercial, throw it on social media, and it will become viral. Or the old story of, "Well, I know a high school kid who makes videos, so I'll just get he or she to do mine." You see a lot of this at the local level where production isn't invested in or is greatly discounted. If you want to have a great product, you must invest in your marketing production.

In looking at production, this book is more about marketing and not the technical side of production, but let's talk briefly about cameras, lighting, and audio. Lighting is very important. If the lighting is poor, it's going to look dark or cast a shadow. If the audio is poor—like in an automobile commercial where there's some guy standing outside in front of the dealership, shouting at a camera, and the audio is muffled because of the wind—it doesn't reflect well on that business because it looks cheap, and it *is* cheap. Remember high production value can and will set you apart.

Earlier, we talked about being the best or different, and there are two main ways to differentiate yourself. Production can make you seem like you're the best or seem bigger than you are versus your competition. The price of building content has come down in price too often. No longer do you need to have film and larger crews. Technology is made available for even the smallest mom-and-pop business to at least compete digitally with the major brands, but they have to make sure it's quality, and the cost is not as expensive as you might think it would be. Again, we're not getting into the technical aspects of pricing in this book, but don't skimp on production.

Timing. When we talk about content, this is going to get more technical, but there are really three calendars you need to look at in creating content. First, pay attention to the world calendar, including holidays and other big events. Second is *your* calendar. What do you have going on in your business? What are the quarterly earnings days or big sales days or Black Fridays? Are there Cyber Mondays? What are the big days in your industry? Third, are opportunity calendars. What do you not know that's going to happen, that you need to be prepared for, should an opportunity jump at you? A great example of this is Oreo.

A few years ago at the Super Bowl, the lights went out in the arena. Oreo was lauded by many people because within a few minutes of the power going out, they produced an ad on social media that said, *You can still dunk in the dark*, with a picture of an Oreo cookie being dunked into milk. They didn't know that the electricity was going to go out at that football game, yet within minutes, Oreo had content about a cookie being dunked in the dark. It got tons of shares, tons of likes, and tons of brand impressions. It was looked at very positively by the marketing and Ad Age community as, wow, they turned that quickly, and that's because it was great timing.

In the Disney+*Star Wars* spin-off, *The Mandalorian*, an adorable tiny baby Yoda steals the show. As any nerdy *Star Wars* fan would know, the original Yoda is a 900-year-old character in *Return of the Jedi*. Because the baby Yoda we meet in *The Mandalorian* is revealed to be just 50 years old, it makes sense that he's still an infant as his full life expectancy is around 900 years.

But here's what doesn't make sense: years, seasons, and calendars are set by earthly trips around the sun. With no earth in this galaxy far, far away—and all of the light-speeding and planet-jumping—how could there even be a comparable time period to know the age of Yoda, or any *Star Wars* character? It's a paradox that we set aside as loyal fans to be entertained by fantasy lightsabers and sci-fi battles in the fight for intergalactic supremacy.

CONTENT TIMING

In a galaxy much closer to home...

Marketers know that each year brings a new calendar, new budgets, and new opportunities. Getting in front of the coming year with a solid content plan starts with a calendar strategy—one that, from a tactical standpoint, may be easier to lay out than you realize.

In looking at your content, beyond production and distribution, timing can be just as important—if not more so—than the quality and quantity. Let's look at an easy way to plan your timing. We'll call it the "three-column calendar." It goes a little something like this:

In an Excel sheet or a simple whiteboard for planning, create three columns.

Column one is the world calendar, column two is your calendar, and column three is the calendar of opportunity.

1. **Column one** is where you write down all of the worldly dates that call for mandatory content needs. These dates also provide an opportunity to stand out should you take the time to prepare—which most banks do not. For example, column one should start with all "bank holidays." This is usually where you are spending your time creating cling-on stickers for your bank doors and meme-ish social media posts to tell your clients that you are closed for the day.

   You know they are coming, so why not take advantage? Here's an old but great example from Central National Bank for Presidents Day (https://www.youtube.com/watch?v=QG9odITUUOU) and a list of some items from the Renasant content site (https://renasantnation.com/category/cool-stuff/) to help with some ideas.

   Go through all of the must-do dates of the year and build your content around those dates. Some—like the major holidays—will have multiple opportunities, while others might just need a digital image or social message. There are usually 15 to 20 events on the world calendar to plan for each year, and they are the same. Every. Single. Year.

2. **Column two** is your "you" calendar. These are the dates that are specific to your community or company. That bank birthday you believe you need to celebrate because you're 125 years old. The Watermelon Festival (https://www.watervalleychamber.com/watermelon-carnival) (it's a real thing), your local hotdog-eating contest, BBQ festival, local tour of homes for your mortgage product—and anything else you'll need that is not externally universal. This is where you include most of your community content and public relations opportunities. Most likely, you plan for these each year as well—as well as annual reports and shareholder meetings for your publicly traded companies. Getting out in front of these can make your life as a marketer a lot less stressful.

3. **Column 3.** In *The Empire Strikes Back*, Yoda says, "Difficult to see. Always in motion is the future." This is your column three. The column of opportunity is, in many cases, the column of the unknown. How can you plan for the unknown, you ask? Well, if you have the first two columns covered with prepared content for known events, you can be ready to take advantage when that M&A announcement hits your inbox. Or your company wins a reader's choice award or was selected as the best bank in your region (https://renasantnation.com/best-bank-in-the-south-with-an-eye-on-getting-even-better/).

Don't fall behind by neglecting to plan your message and content for Presidents, Veterans, Memorial, Labor—you name the day. You know it's always coming. If you don't get ahead of it, it may keep you from discovering a creative opportunity that might be your brand move of the year.

If this all sounds pretty simple—it's just preparation and planning after all—it is just that. However, if you plan your content calendar this way, you'll most likely find 40 days, events, and content topics just to get started on columns one and two. You can then backfill with future opportunities. That comes to nearly one opportunity per week for the entire calendar year.

You can be prepared for holiday sales, summer/spring sales, clearance events, or anything else depending on your line of business. So there are three calendars in the marketplace, and your timing revolves around all three of those.

CONTENT OPPORTUNITY

A lot of brands today look at protecting the brand versus the opportunity. And there's a lot of times when brands can take advantage of the opportunity versus trying to protect some IP that doesn't benefit the consumer, which is the end game to create attention and get the marketing across for sales. A great story that is very similar to this would be with the University of Tennessee, which I happened to attend.

CASE STUDY: UNIVERSITY OF TENNESSEE

In early 2019, there was a school in Florida that had a day for kids to wear their school colors to school. There was a student who liked the University of Tennessee and couldn't find any University of Tennessee athletic gear, so he DIY'd a shirt. He took an orange shirt and drew UT on it with a white marker. He wore it to school the next day and got bullied. Kids made fun of him for his homemade shirt. When you live in Florida, University of Tennessee apparel isn't readily available. So, the young man went to school and got bullied, and his teacher took a picture of it, posted it on social media, and it went viral: https://www.washingtonpost.com/lifestyle/2019/09/12/bullied-boy-who-designed-university-tennessee-t-shirt-just-got-free-tuition-college/.

The University of Tennessee created a copy of the shirt, sold more than 112,000 shirts, and raised $952,000 for the cause of stomp out bullying. They took the money and created a scholarship, so when the student turns 18, he is automatically enrolled in the University of Tennessee with all of his books, tuition, and other expenses paid for.

What they could've done is looked at that kid and said, "Please, cease and desist. Do not make our brand look bad by hand-drawing it on a shirt. Please pull it off social media. We have certain brand standards that we need to uphold in our marketing." Instead, they embraced it, made the handwritten shirts, sold them, and endeared themselves to the masses.

With this, they started anti-bullying campaigns, got a scholarship for a child, and created a whole narrative into how a major athletic brand and university can really absorb social media and take advantage of a content opportunity.

Brand protection is important; you don't want to ever devalue your brand. However, in today's quick-reaction society on social media, too many brands overprotect their brand. The reason is, if I'm ESPN, for example, and I control the broadcast rights to an MLS soccer game, who's to say someone can't pull out their phone, video a great play, save it, and text or tweet it to all of their friends? You didn't ask permission from the MLS, you didn't ask permission from ESPN, but yet it might get 100,000 views.

People see it and think, *I want to go to that game, and I want to experience the excitement that I saw that person have.* Yet big brands say, well no, we own that content. Please take down that video. I'm not saying the MLS or ESPN did that, of course; that's just an example. But the idea is that overprotection sometimes limits brand reach, especially in modern marketing. When a phone can shoot the same video, not production-wise, but the same video content-wise that a brand might protect, if they would embrace it and say, "Look, we want you to shoot our content. We want you to promote our product," then unless they're doing something negative with it, they should just leave it alone. I see that brands often overprotect content, especially when it's consumer-created content that can go viral if they would just let it.

The Walt Disney Company found itself on the end of a content protection overreach and potential PR backlash when a California elementary school screened the Lion King without paying for broadcasting rights: https://www.latimes.com/entertainment-arts/business/story/2020-02-07/disney-pta-licensing-lion-king.

Although Disney had a legal argument, when a big corporation goes after an elementary school for holding a PTA fundraiser around the viewing of your content, it's not a good look. Fortunately, Disney CEO Bob Igar caught wind of the story, reversed the legal recourse, made a personal donation to the school and made a quick PR save. Moral to the story, with mass intimacy and today's easy use of distribution, brands need to choose their content control battles wisely.

Another content example of brand protection versus opportunity was when we did a merger in 2012. Renasant bought into a market that had had a run of banks being acquired often. A bank that was competing with us took out an ad in a newspaper called, "Lost Your Bank," and it had a girl in the ad that had a frown on her face—a really sad, young girl. The copy said, "If your bank has changed names, or if you can't find your bank, we've been here the whole time." And then had a bunch of copy about what their bank values were.

We had a branch manager call and say, "Hey, this bank has taken out a negative ad toward us because they know that we're changing the name of this bank we acquired. They're putting an ad out saying 'lost your bank' with this sad-looking girl in it."

Now, we could've called the other bank and said, "Hey, you're being negative and aggressive with us; please don't do that." This would have looked like sour grapes. Or we could have tried to do something negative back. But instead, we decided that this was an opportunity to match this kind of marketing and really get noticed in the marketplace. So, we got a girl that looked similar to the one in the ad, but she was smiling instead of frowning. Our ad said, "Found My Bank." At the bottom, it said, "If you feel like you need a bank, it's here. We found it."

We played off their copy with our own similar copy but were super positive versus negative. Then we got with the newspaper and placed the ads near each other. People saw the sad one before the happy one, and the ads looked just similar enough. Needless to say, they stopped their ad campaign, and within one week, they took their campaign down. It was a content opportunity, a little bit of creativity, and a little risk to mimic an ad. But it was similar enough that the consumer saw it and said, "There's a play going on here." Of course, that bank took it down because it made us look so positive, and they looked like a sad bank.

CASE STUDY: DWAYNE WADE AND BUDWEISER

Another example is Dwayne Wade and the Budweiser ad on his retirement tour. You would expect it to be about sports, but they did a well-lit ad with the light from a scoreboard cascading over him. Anheuser-Busch brought in families that he had donated money to, some of them anonymously, through organizations that he supports. They all gave him a "jersey." For example, if he had paid for a kid's team to have a jersey, they gave him their professional jersey. Or a lady who got a job gave her business jacket as the jersey for her new job. He had supported all these folks, whether known or unknown to him, through some financial form over his career.

The ad came out with him doing all that, and, at the end it's a thank-you from Budweiser. It didn't talk about beer, and it didn't talk about fun times drinking with your buddies or going to basketball games. It was about a person, the good things he did, and Budweiser saying thank you, Dwayne Wade, for being a part of the Miami community. The interesting part about it were the analytics. The ad agency said that Budweiser sales in Chicago (where he was from) and Miami increased during the ad campaign because people were recalling it, and they were seeing the benefit of Budweiser and their athlete being a community-involved person versus just a beer that you drink with your buddies. That's a good content play on something you wouldn't expect.

It was a social media piece when he walked out on the screen, and people thought LeBron James or Kyrie Irving was going to walk up and thank him. But it wasn't. It was families of everyday people that looked like anyone you'd see on the street anywhere in the world. These strangers were thanking him for his generosity during his career and giving him a "jersey" in their life.

Here's my tie from a businessman. Here's my mortarboard and my gown from graduation because you helped with a scholarship. Wade is crying, and it's beautiful. Budweiser sees a lift in their sales, and it's by nothing other than showing good community work through an athlete who's well-loved in those markets.

When looking at content, produces do not always have to be the feature to be successful. The benefit needs to appeal to the emotions and backfill with logic. These stories appeal to emotion. The friendly girl likes her bank, so that's got to be better than the sad girl at her bank. The Budweiser ad promotes Dwayne Wade as a community person and says Budweiser is part of my community. It doesn't talk about drinking or using their product—it talks about being part of the community. It benefits the community, the technology that enhances your lifestyle, or a friendly-looking bank versus a sad-looking bank. All those are benefits of happiness, time saved, and enormous efficiency in your lifestyle. It all plays into convenience, and if your content can deliver that, you'll win.

When you're looking to create good content, a great way is to look for themes. What's the direction going to be, and where do I look for it? A great place to look is the Super Bowl. That might sound a little cliché or funny, but it's at the beginning of the year. It's when the most money is spent on ads. It's the most money spent on *content*.

Those ads cost anywhere from $1 million to $5 million—and that's not the placement, that's the production value they're putting into them. You see celebrities, voiceovers, crazy animals, CGI, and all kinds of effects. Super Bowl ads are a great place to acquire a big content theme for the year. A few years back, it was all about politics, and it was shunned by some of the critics. Then it went to comedy. All the ads were funny and didn't have anything to do with value or benefit. It was like, here's a funny ad, and here's our brand at the end.

Australia did a fake movie trailer that made a lot of people want to see the movie, then they realized it was just a tourism spot for Australia. But it set the tone that celebrities were going to be making cameos. If you are looking for content direction, don't copy, but think of what is relevant and play to the marketplace. The Super Bowl is a great place to look.

Also, when looking at your content, you should think like a media company—not like a bank, car dealership, plumber, shoe company, etc. Think like a media company because you have to place your content into the marketplace, and media companies do that well. You may be really good at making cars, but that doesn't get attention for your car. You may be a really good bank, but that doesn't get attention for your bank. Thinking like a media company does. How do I make the production right? How do I place it right for the channel? How do I get it into the market-place? A media company would do it much better than thinking like the business you are in. So again, try to look at things as if you are a media company. What should you do to get eyeballs on this marketing?

A popular thing to look toward now is creating a content studio and having staff within your business actually build content rapidly. Marriott Hotels has a content studio where they make all types of content about when people travel, the benefits of staying in a Marriott, etc. You're going to these great locations, you're having great food, and you're having great experiences with your family. Knowing that experience has to be conveyed through content, they create a content studio that's always building new content for the market.

TACTICAL TAKEAWAYS

The Great Eight of Content Marketing

1. **Professional.** This is high-quality production, high-quality audio, high-quality video. It needs to meet a brand standard and be received in the marketplace as very professional. If your production is not great, even though your product is, you might lose the message and your audience. So number one, it must be professional.

2. **Don't be cheap on your production.** Make sure it's high quality, as there are many aspects of production that, if you want your brand to be seen and taken seriously, your production needs to match your brand positioning. You can see startups that have just as good a production on social media as major brands. So don't skip on the production.

3. **When you look at your content, what is the unseen benefit?** If you make fun of something, is there a group that's going to get angry? If you give a price, does it give your competitors your price? If you're partnered with a group that is producing something plastic, could an environmental group get mad at you? If you're backing a group that is not liked for some political reason, could someone get mad at you and hurt your brand? Always look for the "unseen" in your content. Be prepared and plan to address that as it happens.

4. **Value, value, value.** Your content has to give value to the consumer. Otherwise, why are they looking at it? It

can be a benefit, but what's the value in it? For example, car companies all over-run a promotion where they mail you a key with scratch-offs on a sheet. They say, come down to the dealership, put the key in a car, and turn it. If it starts the car, you can have the car. You scratch off lottery-style sheets, and if the numbers line up, you get a prize. Usually, you'll scratch it off, and the prize will look like it's something really impressive. Then you go to the dealership and show the sheet to them, and they say, "Oh no, try the key." There's a disjointed message, and the consumer is disappointed.

The dealership is trying to drive traffic, but they're not giving any value because you don't get anything of value and you've lost time. Maybe you weren't even trying to buy a car because buying a car, on average, only happens every five to six years. There is some negative value in that marketing. The content you deliver to your consumer has to give them a value at the end of it. It might be that you think it's neat or that it's entertaining or funny or informational, but if it doesn't provide value to the end consumer, it's not going to help your business.

What Can Marketers Learn from High Fashion?

In 1985, a little-known clothing designer needed a boost to get his new menswear line brand noticed. At the urging of his financiers, he called up one of the most famous ad men at the time, George Lois. Lois asked him what he wanted to do, and the designer said he wanted to take a model out on the beach in the Hamptons, put him in preppy menswear, and take a beautiful photograph.

Lois responded, "You're crazy! You'll never become known unless you spend millions and millions of dollars. You won't stand out from the competition because they are doing something similar." (1843magazine.com/style/my-fashion-moment/ tommy-hilfiger-on-a-game-of-hangman) Substitute the little-known designer for most bank brands and—just like the conventional fashion marketing approach of putting a model on the beach in clothing—bank marketing tends to all look and feel an awful lot alike.

If you don't think so, and using financial services as an example, visit YouTube and search bank commercials. Could you replace the closing logo with any bank logo and find the commercial about the same for any bank brand? Does your bank's commercial have a strong handshake, open-for-business signs, shots of a young couple and an older couple—and a clean teller row with smiling faces? Perhaps you decided to "take a chance" and have a drone shot over one of your branches or the city or countryside that matches your market, as the flowing feel-good John Tesh-style music fades away. You go, you risk-taker, you.

If you are still doing print ads, does your copy talk about trust, your people, and being part of the community? Do you have bankers that look ready to set a screen in a basketball game with a suit on? Do you talk about how old you are? About how, as times change, you can be there for your clients every step of the way? How you have amazing clients who testify to how great your service is for them?

Much of this same messaging and styling now bleeds over into social media, digital, and web—where banks can interchange a logo on their ads, and no one would likely know the difference.

Let's be honest, these are all correct for banks. There is nothing fundamentally wrong with any of this. It is very comfortable brand messaging, especially in a conservative industry that is bound with product parity and regulatory restrictions. But for bank marketers, if this stings a little and hurts your feelings, welcome to the pity party! As I type this, I'm feeling the exact same shame-of-sameness as you. Guilty as charged for many years.

By now, you've likely nodded to the narrative of a lack of differentiation in bank marketing and are wondering: How do we move away from being just another "model on the beach"? First, start thinking like a brand and stop thinking like a bank.

Banking is a commodity, and we can rightfully assume the general public understands the basics of what a bank does. No, that doesn't mean stop financial literacy or your efforts to bank the unbanked. Those are super important. However, you have something unique about your brand. (If not, you need to go find it.) Take a fresh look at yourself as a brand and try to forget being a bank for just a moment.

In this, realize your brand has certain innate traits that set it apart. For example, our bank, Renasant, is cool, fun, and Southern—because we are based in the South (duh). Our tagline is "Understanding You," which represents our empathy towards our clients.

Now, before you roll your eyes, here is how we set ourselves apart with our brand: We create content that is cool, fun, and Southern that reinforces our brand's personality and connects with our regional audience. And we do this without talking about products or people. And most of the time, we even do it without photos of handshakes or open-for-business signs. Mind-blowing, right?

Examples of this can be found on our content site (renasantnation.com), and—more specifically to our brand traits of being southern and fun—with content about southern football and life in the south; cool—with content about cool things people are doing; and empathetic—with content on our community service (we couldn't escape these stories). Find your brand message and own it.

Second, realize you have more channels at your disposal than at any other time in human history. Not being able to afford TV ads might actually be a good thing when you can just take your message to the people through social and digital channels. All of your content can be sliced and diced for the audience of each medium. And while you're at it, strip the audio and written copy to create audio and blog messaging, as well. With all the modern channel options available, one piece of content can be distributed in many different ways. Find your audience channels and own it.

Finally—because my favorite college communication teacher said you can only get three ideas across in a content piece—my third point is that you have to take some risks to get noticed. It can be humorous like First Bank of Denver's messaging (youtube.com/watch?v=sx-Q2XedC7Ts), or get-it-done cool like Minnwest Bank's "DOers" campaign (minnwestbank.com), or original personal banker branding like Natalie Bartholomew's Girl Banker (thegirlbanker.com). "Dare to be different" is a cliché, but one that banks usually dare to avoid. Find your differential risk tolerance and own it.

To reiterate: Act like a brand and not a bank in finding your brand message. Take advantage of the channels available to your content. Take some compliance-approved risks to set yourself apart from that homogeneous *First Community State Trust Bank* on the nearest street corner.

Oh, and who was that little-known clothing designer? None other than Tommy Hilfiger. You remember, the guy who rushed to the top of the fashion game in the early '90s with a big crest logo on the lower left side of his shirts and fancy nautical-themed garb. He took Lois's advice and passed on doing the model-on-the-beach shoot. Instead, he chose a "hangman" ad on a billboard in Times Square that—although it seems bizarre by today's marketing standards—was seen as courageous and daring at the time. It accomplished the attention he needed to set him apart from what was expected by the marketplace.

If you want to know the full story of what Hilfiger did to avoid the sea—or in his case beach—of fashion sameness, check out this story that inspired this article (1843magazine.com/style/my-fashion-moment/tommy-hilfiger-on-a-game-of-hangman). And listen to the Marketing Money Podcast (marketingmoneypodcast.com) where we take an even deeper dive into the Hilfiger story and the legendary myth that all banks are the same.

5. **It must make sense:** When the consumer sees it, it must show a benefit. If you're explaining, you're losing. If someone has to Google the ad or the product to see what it's really about, you've likely lost them, and, you guessed it, no more text time. Make sure it's simple and can be conveyed through professional production in your content.

The content needs to be accurately portrayed and be correct in the sense that it needs to not be misleading, it needs to be direct, and the consumer needs to know what the benefit is to them.

6. Brevity wins. Five seconds. You have five seconds to get your consumer's attention. Also, "if you're explaining, you're losing." The shorter you can keep your copy or your video, the more you can get your point across while keeping their attention. Don't make what needs to be a two-minute video into a three-minute video. Get the message across with the detail and the benefit and the value to convert, while appealing to emotion. Brevity wins—the shorter, the better.

7. Don't write to an audience, write to a person. The most attention-grabbing word in advertising is "free." The second is "you." Someone who sees free looks for it. Free checking, free oil change, or free dessert with that meal you ordered. Free appeals to their wallet, their benefit of getting something of value for no cost. With this in mind, if you write to a person instead of an audience, they'll be attracted to that direct messaging versus just a broad audience.

You write to "the you" versus "the thing." You often see this mistake with politicians. They will say, "Vote for me, New York"—but there is no New York as a vote. That's a state. (To some, it's a state of mind too.) But it's a person who is voting, not a state. It should be, "I need *your* vote, and "not" I need your vote, New York." Politicians often miss connecting with their audience because they try to talk to a broad electorate versus an individual who has individual needs, and marketing is the same.

You can actually transform your entire content by adding the word *you*. *You* is seen as a connector to someone, like you're speaking to them versus just an audience. So always try to write your copy or create your content towards a person or an individual versus a broad audience. And never underestimate the power of the word *you*.

8. **Be present.** Don't just have a presence. What this means is that if you post something on social media, don't just post it and disappear. When people comment, have an interaction with them and post something in response. Be a brand that breathes and lives in your content. Don't just put up a website and then never check or be available to answer consumers on the contact emails. Don't send the *Do Not Reply* email back to someone when asking them something from your brand. It shows disconnect and disrespect. Always be present in your brand.

It's one thing to have a website. It's another thing to be present on it and interact, whether it be with an active online chat app that can communicate and provide value or someone who can call or text and take care of your needs and offer a benefit for your brand. It's always good to be present with your brand, especially digitally, where people will see your content and interact with it. You need to interact as a brand. Don't just leave it out there for their interpretation over review or over content comments. Be present.

As you look at the great eight things you can do for content, there are also what I call "the hateful eight" of things you don't want to do in your content. Let these serve as warnings of things to stay away from as you produce your content.

The Hateful Eight of Content Marketing

1. **No strong opening or closing.** You have five seconds to catch someone's attention. If you don't come in strong by bringing an emotional tie, a benefit, or value, you're going to lose your audience and become part of the distracted instead of being the distractor. Don't forget the closing—will it convert? Does it tell them how to get to

your product, how to find your product, or what to do? It could be a cause-action campaign. You're asking them to donate. You're asking them to live a certain lifestyle or change what they're doing. If you can't close the message, you've lost as well. Have a strong opening and a strong closing, and make sure you plan for those when you develop your content.

2. **Not building the media for the channel.** If the medium is Snapchat, that needs to be a vertical video, so build it for a vertical video. If it needs to be turned 90 degrees and be a horizontal video for Twitter, or the relaying of the digital website, turn your camera and shoot it that way.

How many times have you seen someone trying to build content, and they shot it incorrectly and made it too long or too short? Understand that if it's Twitter, it needs to be very short. If it's Facebook, web, banner ads, etc., it needs to be built for that medium. Have it prepared to lead them to longer content consumption, but have it built for brevity.

3. **Forgetting that the message is the medium.** The strength of your marketing can sometimes come from where your advertisement is placed. The term "the message is the medium" came to life in the early days of TV. If you're strong enough to be on TV, you must be a strong brand. But it's more than that today. If you're personable, maybe the medium is a handwritten letter. It's certainly not just a blaring TV ad. Today, the message of how strong you are has to be seen with the way it's delivered and the way you process content, not just where you are in the message.

4. **Being a copycat.** Or the model on the beach in our Tommy Hilfiger story. Differentiate yourself. Don't just

build the same content everyone else has seen, or you'll just be part of the sea of sameness.

Look at your website. Could you pull your logo off and put a competitor's on it and not notice a difference? If someone saw one of your videos and it had a competitor's brand at the end, would they know it was you, or would they know it was your competitor's brand? Make sure it's built for your brand and make sure it's built for your messaging. It shouldn't just look like everyone else in your trade.

We see this often in medical marketing. A doctor does one thing, so the competitive doctor does it. The dentist does it, so the other dentist does it. They even name their businesses similarly. We see that in financial services: federal, savings, and community banks all have a similar name, so they don't differentiate themselves. Your name should be different. Don't be the model on the beach.

Another example is banking content. It's almost like they're required to have a handshake shot or a picture of an *Open for Business* sign. If you want to use these same tropes and these same visuals, you're never going to stand apart. Build on your brand and your messaging and own what that is. Don't look like everyone else.

5. **Poor structure, disjointed messaging.** You're trying to deliver a message, but it's disjointed in its delivery. It doesn't convert. You lose people in the message by being too cute. Poor structure can really kill content, so make sure it's structured well to get the message and benefit across, and then everything else should fall into place.

6. **It's funny to you, but no one else.** In all industries, they'll make a joke that's funny because it's part of their vernacular. But outside of it, it means nothing to

the consumer. You're wasting ad space and advertising opportunities.

Be careful of jargon and using language that only makes sense in the business world, but doesn't make sense in the consumer world. A retirement account for somebody might be the beach house account for somebody else. For the bank, it's a college savings plan, but for the consumer, it's the future for their child.

Television shows often place laugh tracks behind the jokes. And if you take the laugh tracks out, they're not that funny, but they try to bring an atmosphere of comedy to make you think the show is funny. And the moment your consumer feels it's artificial or has to be explained that it's funny you're clicking on something else.

7. **Unrelatable messaging.** Copy that doesn't relate to your consumer. It's just too much about the values and not the benefit. It doesn't have an emotional tie. Make sure you hit on the benefit and touch on the emotional reason why the consumer should have your product versus what's important to you and to your industry.

It's also possible to geek out on your product. A great example would be my father going to get his computer fixed, and the person fixing the computer is trying to explain to him all the data he needs, and the memory it takes, and how it has all the latest tech. He just wants his computer fixed. He wants the benefit. He doesn't see the value in more gigs. He got lost in the messaging and felt frustrated. Make sure you're putting forth the benefit and not geeking out on things that are cool to you but don't mean anything to the consumer.

8. **Bad timing.** Not being ready for a certain date or event or not being free to take advantage of a certain event hurts in the opportunity lost department. A great

example is the Pepsi ad with Kendall Jenner with a take on the '60s where she's going to protests and hawking Pepsi as this great unifier of the community. And while it was shot beautifully and done very well as far as production goes, the message was lost because of the timing. There was a real disruption in the US because there were questions of racism and police brutality and a lot of upheaval in the political world.

It made Pepsi look like they were tone-deaf to what was going on in the national conversation. Your product can be great, but if you're tone-deaf, you can damage your brand. Or, at the very least, have a lot of bad spending on marketing because you don't get to capitalize on your investment. Pepsi, one of the strongest consumer brands, remains strong, but still lost valuable advertising resources when they pulled the campaign due to the backlash, especially over social media, they received.

CHAPTER 2
THE SECOND C: CONNECTION

"If it looks good, you'll see it. If it sounds good, you'll hear it.
If it's marketed right, you'll buy it.
But if it's real, you'll feel it."

–Kid Rock

Kid Rock's quote from the inside cover of one of his albums really sums up making a connection through your content marketing. When you connect with an audience, if it's real, they'll feel it. They'll understand it, and they will in turn connect to your brand.

As funny as Kid Rock can be with his style of country, rap, and rock and roll music, he did find an audience to make himself successful because, at the time, his music connected to an audience. Take that into branding and marketing. If people feel and believe that you're giving them a benefit, and if they feel that you are creating an authentic brand that helps them, they will like your brand. Or at least pay attention. They will give you good reviews, they will like your content, and they will become a brand ambassador versus just a person who consumes your content. Again, it can be marketed right. It can be heard. But if it's real and authentic, they'll feel it. And that is connection.

CASE STUDY: HEWLETT-PACKARD

A great example of connection in the marketplace was with Hewlett-Packard's mini-printer ad in 2017. They created a small printer about the size of a cell phone. Hook it up over wi-fi, and it prints wallet-sized Polaroid-style pictures. Hewlett-Packard created a great content spot about three minutes long. It's a story of a father getting up on the first day of school for his sixth-grade daughter. All of the kids are getting ready for school. The sixth-grader acts like she doesn't want to take the picture. He's taking pictures with her on the first day of school, which they've done every year, but it's not cool anymore. She takes the picture, then she leaves for school without saying goodbye. There are pictures of him at work and pictures of his daughter at school. Meanwhile, the mom has downloaded the picture and printed it on the HP printer.

The dad gets home from work and says, "Hey, I'm home." His daughter is playing on her phone, and he walks by, and dramatic music is playing in the background. You can tell he's thinking, *Does my daughter even care? Does she even connect with me?* Everyone is distracted. The daughter is looking at her phone, the mom is preparing dinner, and the dad is walking by some of the children's toys as he goes upstairs. He picks one of them up and brings it to his daughter's room and lays on her bottom bunk to think for a moment. He's having this moment of, *My kids are growing up. Do they care anymore? Are we drifting apart?* Then he looks up at the ceiling of the top bunk and sees that she's taped above her bed those pictures over the years and looks at them every night before she goes to sleep. The dad starts crying, and we almost start crying also, because it's so relatable to parents. His child is growing up, but she still loves her dad.

In the ad, they only show that printer for 1.5 seconds because it's the story of life and holding on to those memories of your loved ones. You cannot watch it and not almost cry, especially if you're a parent. They sold millions of those little printers off this one piece of content alone. It connected with an audience who would want that printer: https://www.fastcompany.com/40462803/hey-parents-feel-like-crying-watch-hps-new-back-to-school-ad.

It's an amazing piece of content that tells the emotional side of being a parent and the awkward teenage years. It showed that the girl valued those pictures with her father every year from the first day of school and everyone since and that Hewlett-Packard's printer was providing the means to that benefit.

Again, we talk about the benefit. You've got to show the benefit, but how does it connect? There is connection in storytelling and how you tell a great story that connects your brand to the consumer.

What snapshots can you turn into a story about your brand? Is it funny? Is it growing up in the South or another easily culturally identifiable part of the country? Is it sports and what the experience is like going to the game? How can you capture those in stories and then connect your brand so that the client recognizes who you are and also cut through the clutter at the same time?

Another great content story that's been going on for years is from the US military. They create content pieces about siblings or family members coming home from serving overseas. These are great content pieces because they touch on the human emotion of "we love them because they protect us." Soldiers come back from their service and there are many emotional hugs.

Content works so well in recruiting for the military because people are seeing it like: *This is the wonderful moment you get after serving, and only people that serve get to experience that kind of moment.* The military has touched on the part of the human essence that says, *I'm protecting my family, and they recognize and they love me*, and they've marketed it well. It is great content marketing for the military.

Connection has to provide value. The Hewlett-Packard ad connected and provided value as a means of capturing that life moment. The military captures an emotional moment and uses it to show the value of your service. You have to include value in the connection. Why should I connect to your brand? Why should your brand connect to me? When you think about connecting with your content, it has to connect. What connects your brand to the consumer?

Another part of connecting with your content is making sure it touches on an emotion with your consumer. The joy of driving a convertible down the coastline is a benefit, but that's also joy in a person's life. They've experienced the success of affording this car to drive it down the coastline; it's an experiential moment. So is the emotion of a wedding and having your child find happiness. How can your brand show this moment and have it relate to and touch that emotion?

Find the heart in your product. As we've mentioned earlier, appeal to emotion, backfill with logic. The logic is the value, emotion finds the benefit. If it's fitting into that dress for the big day, appeal to that emotion with your product. Not that it's stretchy and can't be seen, but that it helps you for that day. That mobile phone that helps you connect quicker and faster to your child or someone you love. That's the benefit. Not that it has this much memory or that it can download this many apps at a certain speed. It's that it connects you to someone, and it doesn't break up or disconnect in the middle of an important phone call. It's important to appeal to the emotion rather than having the greatest and latest technology.

When looking at connecting, let's get a little deeper into what can help with connection: the name of your product or organization. An industry that I work in, financial services and banking, has a huge problem with the name of their organizations.

According to Hunter Young of the Mabus Agency and his research, as well as the FDIC and their naming lists, 62% of banks share a common word in their name: https://www.linkedin.com/pulse/whats-bank-brand-name-today-much-hunter-young/. You're in an already commoditized industry that's conservative in nature and highly regulatory, and yet you're going to choose a name with a word or words that 70% of your other competitors have in their name? That's not good for connection—or anything else, as a matter of fact. But community, federal, state, a direction, (Northwestern federal bank)—you're using names and words that are "bankerly" that sound good and feel correct, but everyone uses those names. You're stuck in sameness.

Examples such as Renasant, Umpqua or the newest name in banking, Truist, are unique names that help set those brands apart. If you're First Bank or Community Bank or South State Corner Bank or whatever, you don't have a unique name. If you're an Ag Credit Union, whatever you are, you've got a name that is very homogenized, and it's going to be hard to set yourself apart when connecting with an audience. On a side note, if you're searching for First Bank of Colorado and there are 102 First Banks coming up in the search engines, you might get the wrong First Bank. You might actually open an account at the wrong bank online. Look at the name of your company; should you rebrand?

Google sounds funny, but it connected because of what it did and was a unique name. So look at the name you have, and how you're going to name your company. If you're small and just starting out, or if you're large and you have an established name, look at your product names. How can you set them aside from others in the marketplace? Then, how can you become the name that's synonymous with the actual product, such as Xerox or FedEx? People say, "I'm going to FedEx it," or "I'm going to make a Xerox of this," instead of "I'm going to mail this or copy this."

While you might be using Bing or Yahoo, it's become part of the vernacular to use Google when mentioning a search engine. This is when your product has become the thing you do versus the name of the company. Some say, "Do you have any Kleenex?" instead of "Do you have a tissue?" because that brand name is now the action of the item you need.

CASE STUDY: POLITICAL TAGLINES

When you look at connection, one way that brands connect with their audience is through a tagline or slogan. It must quickly grab the attention and get your message right into the consumer's mind or into their set for consumption. One lesson, taglines should be five words or less. The Ultimate Driving Machine—BMW. Just Do It—Nike. These are the ones that are always used in brand discussions, but they've gotten it right. They have a value or a benefit that's portrayed and are action-oriented.

At Renasant Bank, our tagline is *Understanding You*. We want our clients to know we understand them and that we're going to meet their needs. We don't talk about, "This is the checking you need with the interest rate you want," or "This or that bank product can do this for you." We just want to understand our clients and meet their needs, which builds a relationship. To connect, write a tagline that is action-oriented and five words or less that compels the consumer to interact with your brand, and that meets a need. Looking at this, let's diverge from business and marketing to politics for a bit.

The great taglines of the past forty years in politics are always remembered, and not just because the candidates won, but because the best taglines actually won as well. You have to be well-funded, you have to hit a note with a national narrative, and timing is important—but a great tagline endures. It's *Morning in America*, Reagan; *A Thousand Points of Light*, George Bush; *It's the Economy, Stupid*, Bill Clinton; *Compassionate Conservatism*, George W. Bush.

No matter what your politics are, if a line works, and it's a good slogan, it will carry forward. Look at Donald Trump's *Make America Great Again*. You can love him or hate him, but as a marketing case study, that is a good brand position because he appealed to conservatives who wanted to make America what they felt it should go back to being. By saying *Make America Great Again*, it appealed to a certain electorate.

Take a look at those who didn't win in politics. Mitt Romney, John McCain, Hillary Clinton, Jimmy Carter, Mike Dukakis, and the list goes on and on. Can you name a tagline from their campaigns? You probably can't, but you can remember Obama's *Hope and Change* and Clinton's *It's the Economy, Stupid.* Those stick in your mind because they were short, they were to the point, and they were great taglines that carried the message for their campaigns.

UNDERSTAND YOUR CONSUMER IN YOUR CONNECTION

Empathy. The best brands show empathy. Empathy is the strongest word in connection with brands, too. If you can't show empathy, there's almost no reason to exist unless you're just utilitarian. We don't need empathetic mops for my house in order to clean it. We don't need empathetic lawn mowers or plungers. But empathy is very important in brand marketing, and it's the key to connection. If you're looking at the heart, emotion, and empathy—and you can connect those to your brand and then convert people at the end—you've created a very successful brand message.

OBSTACLES TO AVOID—DON'T BE NEGATIVE: 10 CONNECTION WRITING RULES

Don't wait in line at the bank, it takes too long. Okay, you just told me not to come to the bank. Don't go down there, you'll get ripped off by the used car salesman, come to our used car lot. Well, you just said "used car salesman," which is a stereotype of someone who's not trustworthy. Marketers need to write positive copy, so avoid starting the sentence with the word *Don't*. *Don't get ripped off.* Avoid starting a sentence with negative words. You shouldn't do this. *Don't miss out.* I know those are action-oriented, but they're also negative, and it makes you think, *Well, I shouldn't be doing that.* Write about the positive side of things, especially in industries that have a history of having ups and downs. That can include medicine, healthcare, banking, government, and politics. If it's had ups and downs, avoid negativity and convey a positive message with your lead sentence.

Here are ten connection writing rules. When you're looking at your connection, there are also obstacles to avoid. One major obstacle in today's world is making sure your IP is free to use and hasn't been used by someone else.

CASE STUDY: HAFOD HARDWARE

By now you've probably heard of Hafod Hardware—a locally-owned store in Wales—because of its viral commercial, which many in the media have dubbed the "best Christmas ad of the year."

It's a homespun content piece featuring a two-year-old living out his day as the owner of an old-fashioned hardware store. It's super cute, and many in the community banking space can relate to its wholesome message of small-town values and hard work. I've even had a few of my fellow marketers ask me how our brand could put together an ad like this: https://www.youtube.com/watch?v=pDtCXO71FJU

In addition, the media reported that it cost Hafod only $130 to make the video. With millions of views, that is a ridiculous return for their brand even before the cash register has rung up any sales. The mere fact that I'm writing about a small-town hardware store in Wales is a tribute to the virality of this content.

How does this translate to what you do?

As marketers, we need to step back, take a look at this digital content, and think about what's behind the curtain. If we feel a little defensive when someone asks us why we can't do that ad—well, that's to be expected. But here is your response:

That ad is great, and we love it. However, it is dangerous as a content piece for a few obvious reasons that any marketer should be able to see quickly.

Before we start dissecting the content piece, let me assure you I am super jealous of the attention it received. I think that it was beautifully done, and I hold the production value of the spot in high regard. Now, let's squeeze those sour grapes.

The song, which really makes the ad, is a cover of Alphaville's 1984 hit, "Forever Young." The artist who covered it, Andrea von Kampen, gave away her terrific cover at no cost other than the $130 to produce the track in a studio. While we have no idea whether Hafod Hardware had permission to use the music from Alphaville—and they very well might have—it would have to cost more than $130 to license it unless Alphaville generously gave it away as von Kampen did. As much as we applaud von Kampen, and potentially Alphaville, for giving away a great song to help a small-town mom-and-pop business with its Christmas advertising, don't expect your bank to receive free music licensing anytime soon.

Even more concerning: at 1:08 in the video, there is a container with Dumbo, Winnie the Pooh, Spiderman, Captain America, Simba, and a few other characters in the shot. It's a cute picture of children's toys, and it plays well with the story. What we're uncertain of here is how well Disney would play along with the use of its IP and characters being used in an advertisement for a non-Disney business. Disney is probably willing to let this go and not be a big bad corporation picking on a little beloved small-town store, but don't count on that for your bank. The mouse paid a lot of money for those properties. Letting them be used for free was probably not the plan in mind when buying the likes of Marvel's cartoon and character catalog.

Beyond the IP issues, the production value of the piece is just too good to be a $130 video. Someone had already sunk the hard cost of what appears to be Red camera footage and great lighting, as well as the expertise to set it properly—along with some really great editing. My four-year-old, who is two years older than the child in the video, cannot sit still to take even one family photo, much less act for a two-minute content piece. That two-year-old is either an incredible young actor or someone is a great editor. I think it's more likely the latter. Either way, someone edited this for free. Plus, the family business didn't have to pay for actors because they played the parts themselves.

The point is, this ad reflects a lot of donated labor and equipment if it really only cost $130. That's a great deal for Hafod Hardware. But it's a bad deal for us marketers trying to convince our bosses for more production and content dollars for 2020.

One could say that relationships matter, and in the case of this Christmas spot for Hafod Hardware, their relationships—and someone's videography skills—paid off in a deeply-discounted content win.

As much as relationships matter, however, so do IP protections. I love the ad and hope it makes millions for Hafod Hardware, but there is plenty here that should give pause to brand marketers wanting to compare this effort to their own content marketing. It's a bah-humbug message wrapped in a Merry Christmas story, but it's one you need to know.

Be Careful with Intellectual Property

Today, there are companies who will run bugs and programs that go through websites to find tagged photos that belong to someone or that they've purchased so then they can send you a cease and desist and a letter asking you to settle with them out of court. It's become a cottage industry. Brands and content creators, especially for the connectivity, need to realize you have to cite properly or purchase the photo and IP properly.

As an example, a fellow marketer told me a story about once needing a stock-type photo for their website. There was a picture of a doorknob that had no artistic value. It could have been taken with any mobile phone or camera and was used to show a story about winterizing your home and closing doors (I don't recall the specifics of the content). His company had to settle for nearly $30,000 with the person who actually took the innocuous photo and owned the rights to the picture, and he had no defense for why he used it for free. When you're creating content, be aware that you have to buy pictures if it's stock footage. Don't just use stuff that you clipped with a tool off the internet because you can get yourself in a lot of trouble.

Be careful when you're making presentations and you're using stock footage, but you haven't taken the watermark off because sometimes that can be leaked out by accident. Even if it was just a holder photo, you have to be very careful. With music, Pond5 is a great company. It does tons of filler music and background commercial music. But be careful about any public ears hearing it before it's purchased because it could create a legal and reputational risk in today's content-heavy marketing world.

Another item in content connection that you need to be aware of is turning off the ability for your competition to place ads on your YouTube videos, especially if you're going to be a heavy content provider. We found this out the hard way. We made some great stories of content about the communities we serve and also the nonprofits we bank with tear-jerker stories about veterans' suicide prevention that we helped fund. We produced one about homeless pet care—folks who can't afford care for themselves, much less their animals. We made these great stories and distributed the content on over social and digital channels, where they were being viewed by hundreds of thousands of people. Our brand mark was at the beginning and at the end. After a couple of weeks, we noticed there were other bank ads for pre-roll, post-roll, and internal roll during our shows. What we found was we did not turn off the external ability for someone to buy an ad around our shows. Our competition saw the success we were having and the brand impressions we were getting and started buying ads on top of us.

Of course, we turned them off and said, "Glad you noticed. That's awesome." It felt great that someone noticed that we had successful content marketing, that eyeballs were seeing it, and thought it was a good enough medium to buy our show as an advertising medium for their brand that competes with ours. That's a big mistake that a lot of brands make when they post their content. If I'm AT&T, Verizon might buy ads on my show.

If I'm Budweiser, Coors Light might buy ads on my show. Make sure you turn off the ability for the competition to take advantage of your reach and impressions.

In connection, these are all modern challenges that didn't exist before. People weren't parking ads on competing brands on YouTube in the '50s. You couldn't put pre-roll in front of your digital campaigns in the '60s or '70s. We have modern opportunities and challenges that didn't exist years ago, and that's why the four Cs are more important than ever to have a foundation for your marketing mix.

In addition to connection, do not underestimate the power of social media. Many brands are scared because of the feedback they'll receive, or they'll say something tone-deaf, or they won't have the ability to interact quickly enough for today's consumer's expectations. If I posted a complaint about my airline flight, the expectations are, *Why haven't they gotten back to me?* I'm delayed because rideshare didn't get there in time. *Why are they not getting back to me?* But you have to be prepared for that because there is no next time if you miss with your consumer. They'll fly American instead of Delta. They'll choose Lyft instead of Uber if you don't give them the connection experience they think they deserve. They'll complain about it over social media, or, if you provide a great reaction meeting their expectations, they'll promote you over social media, and you'll get a high net promoter score, or a four or five-star review. What we've got to look at is social media as a connection tool is probably, in today's modern media mix, the number one way to interact with your consumer beyond person-to-person non-digital interaction.

A great example is the airline industry. How quickly can a person pull out their phone and video a bad experience? All of a sudden, you've got a reputational risk, you've got negativity instantly on social media. Many airlines have become really good at responding quickly to Twitter or Facebook with their social media tools. For example, Delta does a really good job of interacting with you quickly on Twitter. If you post something such as *My flight's delayed* or *I've missed my connection,* they're actually faster to reconnect you over Twitter than they are over the phone or even in person. They've taken advantage of the reach of social media to make their customers happy. As negative as it can be, it can be a positive medium for your marketing team as well.

When people think of digital, they often think of just social media, but we're talking web experience. The Internet is one place where there's a lot of disconnection in advertising. You'll see an ad that says *Get this widget here*, and then it'll take you to a home page that has nothing to do with the specific widget that was offered in the advertisement. Companies should consider micro-siting, which is taking the consumer to the specific thing they were looking to find. If I'm looking to buy a jacket and I click on your digital ad, don't take me to a general page, take me to where I can get that jacket, pick the size, and make the purchase with ease.

If I'm trying to buy a car, and I click on a car ad, take me to that specific car I saw, don't take me to the dealership advertisement on a web page. Make it specific to the client experience and what they're looking to buy because they will click right off if you don't take them to what they were browsing originally.

An example of this is North Face, who reintroduced their Denali jacket. When they did, they delivered digital ads - mostly placed in an outdoors article - or over social media. When you clicked on their ads, it took you straight to a micro-site that was the exact jacket you clicked on earlier. All you did was choose your color, your size, and then you checked out, and it was sent and delivered after choosing your delivery time. They got that consumer to see it, had that emotional five seconds to really hit that interaction, and then the consumer clicked to the right area. Boom. Success.

We've talked a lot about digital, web, social media, and connection; however, don't forget about traditional advertising. There's still a market for print. There's still a market for direct mail, maybe, ha. There's still a market for television. If you have a more senior demographic for your product, *Wheel of Fortune* in the evening or the evening news is a great medium for advertising.

If you have a younger demographic, direct mail actually works for young people because they don't get as much mail. I think it's often forgotten that a 16-year-old doesn't get a lot of mail, and if you have a product that typically appeals to a 14 to 20-year-old demographic, it may really work.

To Gen Xers and Boomers, mail is kind of like, *Eh, I've gotten so much over my lifetime.* It's junk mail for a reason. But to the new consumer, they don't get a lot of mail, so it's different. Think of using traditional mail in a different way for a demographic that it might actually appeal to because they don't see it a lot.

Other connectivity in traditional mail would be something that's called "lumpy mail," where you make a weird-shaped item in the mail to make them open it to find out what it is. Also, bright colors that are different from a traditional white envelope, the oversized postcard, or the pop-up mail piece that's 3D. Some of this is overplayed. It's been done so much now that it often falls into the junk mail category, but the most important part of direct mail is your list.

In direct mail, the list is most important. Eighty percent of the response will be based on the list and offer because a good list is who has the propensity to convert. The other factors ranked are 10% on creative and 10% on timing.

INFLUENCER MARKETING

In modern marketing, we also have influencers. Traditional influencers might be a corporate spokesperson. You hired a famous athlete to represent your brand or a famous news broadcaster or a Hollywood movie star. That would be more of a macro influencer, and they did not own their audience. Now, we have micro-influencers on Instagram who push a product every day. Be careful of influencers. The FCC has recently put out guidance on using influencers that they need to disclose that they're paid for their product: https://www.ftc.gov/news-events/press-releases/2019/11/ftc-releases-advertising-disclosures-guidance-online-influencers.

But influencers' connectivity can be a great marketing asset, depending on your product. I'm a 40-something-year-old white male. I probably don't relate to the 16-year-old female, but finding a 16-year-old female who has a million followers on Instagram in the markets we're in might be a good marketing plan if our brand seeks that demographic. Influencers can be effective, when they're the right fit for your brand's target. Also, realize there are reputational risks with influencers because they can go do anything they want versus a brand that has regulatory protections, insurance, and legal protections and check-offs, however, influencers offer an opportunity to present your brand to demographics you might not be able to reach otherwise.

CASE STUDY: GARY VAYNERCHUK

Connect with Content Distribution
Bestselling author, entrepreneur, and marketing personality Gary Vaynerchuk has done a very good job of content marketing for himself and his business. Vaynerchuk has millions of followers, he speaks all over the world, and knows a lot about content. When he talks about it, he has eighty different ways to use one piece of content, and it's a really take on modern content delivery: https://www.slideshare.net/vaynerchuk/the-garyvee-content-model-107343659.

He says, "If you record a video, strip the audio, use it for a podcast. Strip that as copy for a blog post. Strip that as an email message to your followers. Then have a place for them to subscribe and push your videos back to them. Cut your video up. If it's an hour-long seminar, cut it up into little five-minute segments, and then take a minute of that and put it on social. Have the minute lead to five minutes. Have the five minutes lead to the full presentation. And so take your content and chop it up to where you can hit all types of areas. It could be that you do a print ad from the picture of your presentation in a print piece or on a billboard. Then flip it back to social media with a tweet. Then take the copy from that and turn it into a podcast. Take the audio and turn it into even a voicemail message." You can take content and cut it up to connect with your audience on the medium in which they choose to be connected.

If you haven't heard of Gary Vaynerchuk, he started Wine Library and was one of the first people to really use Google as a marketing mechanism when he was buying ad words at pennies on the dollar. For example, today you may be paying $20 or $30 a keyword, if not more, depending on the pricing of your keyword. Vaynerchuk propelled the Wine Library become an internet sensation by making YouTube videos explaining wine and the value of different wines you buy. And he figured out that content was more than just wine. It was whatever you wanted it to be if you did the production right, the delivery right, and had an honest message. He's cultivated this personality of being a wine expert on winelibrary.com into now doing it for a lot of brands by coaching them on how to reach the consumer through content and connectivity with their brand messaging.

How to Connect

In connectivity, we must be fluid—as in, be ready to move. You have to be agile in the marketplace today. In the past, when the four Ps were around, it was really easy just to buy a television show, buy one of the four stations, put up a billboard, and buy a print ad. Today, you have to be agile as a marketer because delivery channels are moving quickly.

One must be cognizant of the graveyard of many failed apps and content channels from Myspace to Google Plus to Vine. But new ones arrive just as fast, from Snapchat to TikTok, and by the time this book is published, there'll be even newer ones. When they get into the billions of followers and customers, you can be pretty sure they will stay around. Be mobile and agile and able to move yet be conservative with resources about planning it toward one of the newer mediums until it is more established.

Building a subscriber base is also an important tactic. What happens if you have a million likes on Facebook or a million connects on LinkedIn and that medium goes down? What do you do with all this equity you've built into that social media following? Create your own channel and subscriber list. Have your own site, a content site. Have your own blog or your own vlog or some platform where you can have subscribers and collect that data. Data is today's gold, and if you have data, you can connect with them as opposed to just being beholden to one medium of connectivity. While you can choose one or two and be really good at it, if you can't be good at Facebook, Twitter, LinkedIn, etc., choose one or two and be really strong but have a backup plan to save your connections and brand followers.

As much as we've talked about positive connection—with Hewlett-Packard's HP printer, and some of the other stories we've mentioned—there have been some instances in which a connection didn't happen, and brands have had to kind of rewire the way they communicate with their consumer and the public. Some examples of those are Volkswagen when they had an issue with their emissions testing. Another one is Uber when they had some reputational risks from the CEO down to some of the drivers. And Papa John's when there was what we'll describe as a bad conference call. Plus Domino's, who self-admitted that their product wasn't that great. All of these companies have run what is a combination of an apology and correction tour campaigns. Many brands have perfected the creative approach in their marketing to admit their faults, explain how they are fixing it, and then try to show the benefit of the fix.

Hardee's is another one that would fit into this group. They were missing their demographic on their product and thought their brand had fallen flat. They reinvented it with supermodels eating their burgers because they figured their demographic were men, and that's what they knew they wanted to see from their data. They let their data tell them how to connect. Even though all these brands are really strong brands, they still have really good business models, and they had to make a shift in how they were delivering their message. They apologized, they set it straight, and they connected with their consumers. All of them appear to be doing really well, and you can look at some of these commercials here: https://www.washingtonpost.com/news/business/wp/2017/03/30/carls-jr-sex-no-longer-sells/.

Another important aspect of connecting with your customer is providing an experience. Content can be more than just what people see on their phones. It can be the experience they have. The most successful McDonald's restaurants are the ones that clean their windows and their front door every 30 minutes or even more often. That might play to the bigger picture of an active management role in the company, but they've noted that in their training if you clean your windows and doors, you'll be a more successful McDonald's.

Jimmy John's sandwiches has adopted this as well. They are freaky fast in how they deliver quickly with their product. If you go into a properly managed Jimmy John's, it will have crystal clear windows and doors, and the minute there's a fingerprint, they wipe it clean. In the fast-food industry, it's a differentiator. It is mandatory for Jimmy John's franchisees to log when they clean the windows and doors, and it's created a very successful brand to go along with their fast delivery.

Connection is found through finding the right audience with your content. But it can be more than just digital content. It can be your brand promise, brand value, client journey and overall experience.

TACTICAL TAKEAWAYS

The Great Eight of Connection

1. **Find your audience.** You must know where your audience is and how to connect with them. Is your audience on Facebook? Is your audience watching TV? Does

traditional media connect with them? Connect with your audience where they are, with a remarkable experience, and get to know your audience so that you connect with the heart when you deliver your message.

2. **Buy and sell on emotion and backfill with logic.** Touch the heartstrings. Touch with the benefit that you provide. Backfill it with the value, the price, and how you get it. Appeal to the heart, and you'll win the mind.

3. **Go to the eyeballs.** Use hashtags, look and see who's following you and what's trending on social media. If your brand plays into that, that's where you should place your content. For example, if you have a product that appeals to real soccer moms, why is it not being displayed near the soccer fields? Look where the eyeballs are and place your product near the eyeballs so they can see it. That's where you're going to connect with them.

4. **Use partner reach.** A great story about that is from a webisode we produced called "Crafted." It was a show about entrepreneurs and their businesses. And one we chose to feature in a marketing campaign was ORCA Coolers who created high-end branded coolers. We shot a five-minute piece, cut it up into one minute for social media, and then made a beautiful show about the great ORCA Coolers—how they were branded and how they were made in America. And it just so happened that Brett Favre was an investor in ORCA Coolers: https://renasantnation.com/american-orca-coolers-crafted-renasant/.

We didn't have to pay celebrity rights. We didn't have to pay for his time. He wanted to be there because it was a product in which he was invested. Also, we looked at ORCA and noticed they had a decent social media following. Then, they promoted our content themselves, and the next thing you know, in their stores around the region, they're showing the content piece on the TV screens in their stores with our logo on it. Look for partners who will co-promote with you and look for partners who may have greater social reach to amplify your reach and connectivity.

5. **Market the marketing.** People are always interested in how things are made. Not so ironically, there is even a show called *How Things Are Made*. Look at your marketing and have someone shoot the marketing while you're building it. If you're doing a commercial, build a "behind-the-scenes" and put it on social media. Show how you got the celebrity in it, then put that on social media and on your website. Make a blog about it. Talk about how you made the marketing as much as releasing the marketing into the public.

6. **Engage your internal audience.** If you work for a large company, and many of your co-workers are on Facebook or LinkedIn, when you send out a content piece, send out an internal message. Tell them to promote it. Tell them to like it. You can actually get something to trend if you just have a few thousand people within your own company to promote it and everyone to like it at the same time.

7. **Pick channels and topics with a big following.** If you know something's trending, or if your industry has a big following from a certain person, like an influencer, try to partner up with them. Choose an area that has eyeballs that you can connect with rather than buying television commercials or print advertisements. Find an audience and go chase that audience to create your brand awareness.

8. **Don't be boring.** Even if subjective, nothing's worse than wasting the attention and time of your consumer. Don't be boring. Be exciting. Be funny. Be emotionally grabbing. Be empathetic. But don't be boring.

The Hateful Eight of Connection

1. **Too broad a message or too targeted a message.** Now those might seem juxtaposed, but if your message is too broad—and remember, we talked about writing to a person and not an audience—you won't make specific connections. On the other hand, beware of being too targeted. Yes, it takes balance. If you put an ad or a piece of content out about a purple Martian from this corner of the world that only does one thing, you can't connect with an audience at all. You have to find that median between a target audience that's ready to connect and not too targeted when it's so narrow you have no connection ability.

2. **Content that's not engaging.** It's a huge mistake to put content out there just because you felt you needed to make some content. An example of this was when Verizon hired Jamie Foxx for an ad campaign. They didn't do a lot with Jamie Foxx, they just had him talking, and he didn't really even make any jokes, which is something for which he is known. If you have a great content piece or person or influencer, make sure it engages with your audience, and push it to engage them to do business with you. Don't be lazy with it. Make the content engage with your audience.

3. **Not taking any risk.** Every content piece is a risk. You can be criticized for not being engaging. You can be criticized for it not hitting the mark, but it has to have some risk in it just in being created, so take calculated

risks with your content. Remember our Tommy Hilfiger story? He took a risk by not showing any clothing, and it created a whole brand for him that was different from the other clothiers.

4. **Don't be only about you.** This is one that's true to heart with banking. There are so many ads where customers give testimonials about their services from the bank, but all they talk about is the bank. They don't talk about what they do. They don't talk about the benefit. They just talk about the bank and how this bank is here and how this person helped me. It comes off as very contrived and paid for rather than just focusing on the story of the benefit. Don't talk about yourself, talk about the benefit or talk about what the consumer's connection is to your brand.

5. **Getting too mission-driven and away from your business.** Although goodwill content may win hearts and be a great winner in the "feels" department, don't forget that you are a business, and to keep your doors open, you have to make money. Remember to bring your content around to what you actually do at some point.

6. **Too much following your competition.** Why do the same thing everyone else is doing? Car dealerships, mobile phones, doctors. Following, following, following. Everybody looks the same. Make yourself different and be your own brand.

7. **Disjointed messaging.** When the last *Jurassic Park* movie came out, there was a geo ad campaign that hit where we lived. It placed digital ads with a dinosaur in it, but the ad told you to go to Walmart to get Skittles. I don't know what algorithms put it together that people who watched *Jurassic Park* must shop at Walmart and specifically buy Skittles. However, when you clicked on it, it just took you to Walmart's home page.

It was a very disjointed message. Maybe they wanted you to buy the Skittles to take with you to the movie, and you bought them at Walmart. Maybe that had some algorithm that told them it worked, but the ad campaign was bizarre. It was noticeably different in how disjointed it was because it was three brands rolled together. Walmart wasn't selling the DVD or the movie for *Jurassic Park* because it was brand new. They were trying to play off the name in their sponsorship of the movie to sell Skittles. It just didn't make sense. As you look at your content, make sure your message easily cuts through the clutter and gets to your consumer versus creating both market and brand confusion.

8. Not having copy that connects your message.
Copywriting is a lost art. You've got to make sure that your copy connects to your audience.

If you can't connect to your audience, your content is worthless. You can have the greatest videos and the greatest messaging, but if it does not connect to your audience both emotionally and technically, it won't work. You can connect emotionally, but if you can't get it to them technically, they'll never see it. You can get it to them technically, but if it doesn't connect emotionally, they'll never feel it. So you must have both the emotional connection and the ability to get it there, which creates a great connection for your content.

And so to go back to the Kid Rock quote, he understood that if someone hears it, feels it, it's marketed, and it's organic—they will understand it, and it will reach an audience. And he did that with his music at the time to mass appeal. Whether you like him or not, it worked. With content, you have to be able to connect, and it has to touch emotional heartstrings and then have the tactical delivery to get there.

Today's copywriting is very different from the way it was just 15 or 20 years ago. You'd write these long, drawn-out paragraphs that the consumer would read and absorb because they weren't distracted like people are these days with different forms of technology. It was access through reading a newspaper or magazine. There are great copywriters—like David Ogilvy and George Lois, who we mentioned earlier—who were really good at long-form advertising through the written word. If you want to learn the foundations of advertising and copywriting, make sure to read Ogilvy's *On Advertising*. It should be required reading for marketers.

But, today is different from the heyday of Ogilvy. You write for optimization of search terms. You have to write with the idea that someone will search for what you have written. In many cases, sentences and the layout of websites might even look bizarre, but they're written for the web and not for print advertisements. And what's really interesting is that there are some websites for major companies that don't look that great as far as aesthetics, but the copy and layout is built so that you'll be found quickly on Google, Bing, Yahoo, or any other search engine.

Storytelling in print is not as effective as it used to be as it's moved to video. You need to write for a person, not your audience, and you need to write with the idea that someone will be searching for the topics about which you're writing.

A clearer message on a website may be more important than the aesthetics. I love aesthetics. I want a good-looking site. I want it to be clean, easy to find, easy to convert, easy to operate. The message comes across, and it makes your brand look good because of its quality. But if you look at Walmart, Amazon, even some larger banks and bigger companies, they're more built toward SEO—finding a product and selling a product—than they are on giving you an experience on the site. It works for them, and it works tremendously well. I think there's an in-between there. You could make it look better, but the ones that look great may not convert as well. They don't have a shopping basket that's easily accessible that saves your credit card or has some type of digital payment process.

But also know what your audience wants. If they're going on a website to buy toilet paper to be delivered to their front door, I don't think they really care if it has beautiful pictures. They just want the amount, the price, and to click and check out. Build sites for your audience's consumption.

In my experience in marketing, it seems while some marketers are great creatives and producers and great at visuals, a lot of them, or us, have weak copywriting skills. We need some quick lessons and some rules for you to adhere to going forward. The Seven Oxford Copywriting Rules can be pulled out as tactics to maybe put on a sticky note or sheet of paper and put where you can easily see it when you are writing business copy. Know that these will make your copywriting better, even if you haven't had any formal lessons in copywriting.

THE SEVEN OXFORD COPYWRITING RULES

1. **Positive action-oriented tone.** Tell the consumer what you want them to do. Just like when we talked about taglines, they need to be action-oriented. Do you want people to drive the car? Do you want them to understand something? Do you want them to know something? Do you want them to do something? Create an action and make it positive. No one wants something negative. Explain the benefits with an action-oriented tone.

2. **No sentences in prepositions.** This is an old unwritten rule, and today's vernacular has become mangled through shortness and quickness in text messaging. As a result, this ended up creating things like LOL and BRB. Our language has changed. But when you write, it still needs to have some type of formal professionalism to it. When you say, "Where are you at?" or "This is where

we're at," you can get away with it verbally and still be okay. But if it's in formally written advertising copy, it looks unprofessional and may turn people away.

3. **Hyperlink your words.** The difference between older copywriting and newer copywriting is that you can hyperlink words to sites, to conversions, or to anything that gets the customer or your audience to where you want them to go. Don't forget that when you write digitally, if copy is going to be on a website, hyperlink the words, tag them for SEO, tag them to your customer relationship management (CRM) system. Get that click, and you get that data back along with what has been looked at on the site or in the copy. You might see where the eyeballs are going because, if they're clicking on a certain word, you know that it's hitting your audience, and that makes it SEO friendly.

4. **Don't use all-encompassing words like *everything* because it takes away the personalization of the copy.** Write to the person, not the audience. Use words like *you* or *me* versus *everyone* because it needs to be personalized in today's targeted marketing. Ensure your copy is personalized and not overreaching or trying to be too broad in its delivery.

5. **The fewer articles, the better.** He, she, it, the thing, this thing, that thing. Be brief, but be descriptive. When you just say "this thing's a great thing," the repetitiveness of articles that aren't descriptive will lessen the impact of your copy.

6. **The shorter the sentences, the better.**

7. **No absolutes.** *Everyone* loves to go here. *All* people do this. You have to get away from absolutes because, again, that is writing to an audience and not to a person. Everyone might not like this product. All people might not do this certain thing. Avoid using absolutes

and make it specific to an audience of one, and write for them and not the masses. Remember mass intimacy is the new way to connect.

In looking at the Oxford's Seven Rules, they're not all-inclusive. You may have your own rules. Other English teachers may have better rules. But if you're looking at writing for copy—for advertisement copy or advertising copy—these seven rules will help you, especially if you're a Marketing 101 student or just getting into marketing. Maybe you're marketing yourself in your own brand, and you don't have any help. Using these seven rules as a baseline, assuming you already have decent grammar and writing skills, will help guide you toward your goal of professional-looking written copy that can be effective for what your audience is looking to find.

Above all, have a very clear call to action. Your message is so important. While you have values, benefits, and details—there has to be a call of action or you're just rambling. Get the consumer where they want to go so you can convert. Help them to help you!

Even if your site has a great description of a product or has copy that has a great story to tell, it needs to get the consumer where you want them to end up. And it needs to do it in the way *they* want to get there. Microsite, click here, buy here, and go here. Clicking on a product is so much better than making people have to type in a web address or go search for the product after they've read about it. Make sure you have a link or a click that takes them where you want them to go because that's part of the conversion. That gets the content to the connection to the conversion, which takes you through three of the four Cs.

Regarding how to write effective copy in modern marketing, subject lines in emails are very important because you have those five seconds to grab their attention. The subject line is what people see when they're scrolling through their emails. If you don't have an attention-grabbing subject line or something that's at least to the point, that person may not want to know you. If it's a sales-driven email or a connection-driven email, the subject line is the most important thing you have there.

It's like taglines: five words or less and action oriented. Do not put it all in caps so it looks like you're screaming. Do not use different fonts or emojis because then it looks unprofessional. Make sure it gets to the point, is brief, but tells the person what you expect them to take away from your email.

Chapter 3
THE THIRD C: CONVERSION

"Half the money I spend on advertising is wasted. The trouble is, I don't know which half?"

—John Wannamaker.

John Wanamaker was one of the first recognized American marketers. He was the first person to create long-form copy print ads, up to half a page. If you look at old print copy, it's just all words and maybe a little illustration, but heavy copy. Wanamaker was one of the first to skip placing a little ad and instead chose to do half or full pages to grab readers' attention. At the time, it was groundbreaking advertising.

He would make the ads, but he couldn't measure them; he had a conversion problem. He could see that his ad would grab attention. He could hear and see people talking about it and reading it because they didn't have social media or television in the 20s. When he wrote copy, he could not figure out which was the most effective and which wasn't. He knew half of it worked, but he wasn't sure which half.

When we look into conversion with modern marketing, we need to be able to test what works because we have more tools at our disposal than at any time in human history for advertising.

We have social, digital, traditional marketing, television, radio, billboard, direct mail, etc. There are so many options in a holistic marketing plan that you have to decide which one works best for you.

How do you get the most out of your dollar? Is Facebook right for you? Do you get a lot out of boosting Facebook posts, or do you get nothing? Does direct mail work for you? It's very measurable. But what you're measuring doesn't really drive brand, so you have to decide what works for you and what your outcome needs to be.

We must start with the first two Cs to get to conversion. If you don't have content that grabs attention and connects to your audience, you can't convert your consumers because they'll never get to the sale. One mistake companies, politicians, and individual branders make is that they jump into promoting a product before a known brand. Without brand awareness, you could have the greatest t-shirt, soap, or shoes in the world, but greatly decrease your value. That's why branding is so important, especially when you're in a commoditized business such as banking, mobile phones, or cars. If you don't have brand awareness, people aren't just going to use your location unless it's purely out of convenience. If your bank's next to someone's house, they may go into it. But that's about convenience, not branding.

Brand awareness is created through content and connection. Even if you've built the best content, you're connecting with your audiences, you're building followers, you're building connections—you're just doing it all really well. Your management team will still ask, "How is it converting into the bottom line?" That's where the third C of conversion comes in. It is so important not only to have beautiful content and great connection and messaging but to be able to convert those connections into real dollars.

ROI. What is ROI? Obviously, it is return on investment. But it also can be return on integrity, it can be return on many things beyond dollars. Sometimes a brand message might be trying to fix a reputational challenge, which then leads you to create more sales due to goodwill. However, you have to know what return is expected for your marketing. Is it impressions on a video that leads to someone searching for the product to find out what it is?

Let's say I have a direct mail list of 10,000 people, and I mail every one of them. As they buy whatever the widget is, I mark them against the list and run it back and say 2% of my list was activated because that percentage came in and took action on that mail piece that showed up in their mailbox. Direct mail is probably one of the easiest ROI marketing pieces to measure because it's a list with action that you can measure your conversions.

Television is one of the hardest. Unless you have a direct call out in a television ad—a phone number or text, for example—it is really hard to measure television. We can measure the eyeballs through ratings, but you really don't know if it's creating action to convert. Television is a very good branding medium, but as a conversion medium, it's not the best for measurement. Digital, on the other hand, is a good branding medium, but also one of the best conversion mediums as it gives the ability to click through and convert customers. You can then measure how much you spent on digital and what your return is. For example, say I placed an ad and received 1,000 clicks, and out of those 1,000, 300 of them clicked through to the product, and 200 of them finished the journey to complete a transaction by purchasing a product.

That's why marketers are slowly moving away from television as their biggest spend and/or increasing digital in their marketing mix. The ability to convert and measure through digital makes it a great channel for all sizes of business.

In looking at how you measure analytics, one of the big words that gets thrown around a lot in marketing is "big data." It's an overarching theme and really depends on the specific item you want to measure. Again, is it impressions, is it clicks and inter-actions, is it building an audience through a subscription? You may just want to build an audience and connections through followers on Facebook or through LinkedIn. This may lead to the sales funnel you're building to deliver content to connect and then convert.

You definitely must understand your analytics. Not only will this help to understand and track conversions, it will also help you determine your tactics to deploy. When you look at these analytics on your marketing, you need to be able to tell how much was budgeted for it, what the outcome was that you wanted to achieve, and its conversion rate. Then, measure that outcome and continue to make adjustments as needed.

For ROI, take advantage of digital reach. If you get a 30% open rate in an email campaign, you're doing well. Even getting more than 20% is impressive. A decade ago, 80 to 90% of emails were opened, but now it's less than 20%. Again, when doing email, it absolutely has to have an attention-grabbing subject line. Open rate is obviously important in emails during the process of conversion.

Clicking through is important in digital campaigns. Did people click through? How much did they watch of my video content? Did they scroll through it? Did they get to the pre-roll, see your ad, and click to fast-forward through it because it wasn't effective in grabbing their attention? Or maybe it was effective, but they weren't looking for that specific product you were selling. Did they just want to see the video but weren't in the market for your product? You've got click-throughs, open rates, and bounce rates. Do they immediately bounce off when going to the website? Are they not staying on the website because it's not attracting them, or it's not what they're trying to find? That's why you build a content site where they have content they're looking to find.

Also important in conversion marketing is how you keep track of your customers and your audience. Two technical apparatuses that you can use for this is a CRM, which is a customer relationship management system, and an MCIF, which is a marketing customer information file. They are both basically data warehouses. But any marketer should know they're a bit different in that the CRM can tell you who your customers are, where they are, and what they do—maybe even their profitability on what products they have, the share of wallet you have with them, and how many products they have from your company.

The MCIF is how you attract those customers. Is it the campaign, measuring the email, the tagging through cookies that tells you how successful your campaigns are? You have these two databases, and any marketer should have access to these databases and protect them because this data is very important. It's also really important for those clients because they don't need to be hacked. An effective marketer will be able to look at the data and use it to impact their campaigns and optimize for stronger ROI.

Hilton is an example of what a CRM system would be when you check into a hotel. When you check into the Hilton, the greeter says, "Hey, you're diamond status! Welcome back, Mr. Oxford." They'll know you've stayed there previously because their CRM triggers that you've been there before. It also might have some information: likes water in his room, likes the air conditioning at 67 degrees, likes coffee in the morning. A good CRM can help you get this specific. They allow the business to know the customer's preferences before they even get there, which then shows empathy and drives loyalty.

Another great way to use an MCIF in the banking world would be to look at how many checking accounts and savings accounts you have. Compare the two and pull the checking accounts out that don't have savings accounts at your bank. Market savings accounts to those checking account holders. They already trust you, they already know your brand, and they already have a checking account with you.

Deliver messages in an email, digital campaign, or a social campaign to this target audience. Maybe you add in some direct mail for those that you can predict are likely to come into the branch because they're uncomfortable doing it digitally. Or it could be a digital click-through that you built through an MCIF to track conversion and activity. In the end, you can go back and run the list of opens in savings accounts to your original list to get the percentage of opens. And then that's how you create your ROI. Take the costs you put into marketing and the email against the costs an account is valued and that would be how you figure out ROI.

Another great way to convert clients, which has risen to prominence over the last three or four years, is geo-fencing. Geo-fencing is looking at a map or a location of your competitors (which some refer to as geo-conquesting), or areas where you might have a client lead, and dropping digital/social advertisements that are geotargeted that can create native advertisements on social media. It's digital marketing. You fence in an area by circling the area on a map, dropping ads, and tracking who sees it and if they sign up or click there. There are many companies that help with geo-fencing. If you need a quick resource, check out www.rainlocal.com.

MEET THE COOKIE

A computer "cookie" is more formally known as an HTTP cookie, a web cookie, an internet cookie, or a browser cookie. The name is a shorter version of "magic cookie," which is a term for a packet of data that a computer receives then sends back without changing or altering it. No matter what it's called, a computer cookie consists of information. When you visit a website, the website sends the cookie to your computer. Your computer stores it in a file located inside your web browser. (To help you find it, this file is often called "Cookies.")

WHAT DO COOKIES DO?

The purpose of the cookie is to help the website keep track of your visits and activity. This isn't a bad thing. For example, many online retailers use cookies to keep track of the items in a user's shopping cart as they explore the site. Without cookies, your shopping cart would reset to zero every time you clicked a new link on the site, which would make it impossible to revisit preferences online.

A website might also use cookies to keep a record of your most recent visit or to record your login information. Many people find this useful so they can store passwords on commonly used sites or simply so they know what they have visited or previously downloaded.

Different types of cookies keep track of different activities. Session cookies are used only when a person is actively navigating a website; once you leave the site, the session cookie disappears. Tracking cookies may be used to create long-term records of multiple visits to the same site. Authentication cookies track whether a user is logged in, and if so, under what name.

Geo-fencing is the new newspaper advertising. Now, you get your phone, you open it up, and you scroll through it. How are you placing ads onto apps in sites people are visiting?

In a campaign, you might want to geo-fence locations that are mobile-friendly to viewing, such as a hospital or sporting events. For example, if your bank has Affinity debit cards—which is a school logo on a card—you could geo-fence a circle over the football stadium. During the game, you then drop ads on the football stadium, and as fans are scrolling through their phones, they see your ad. They connect your team with their bank, giving the perception that the bank is loyal to their team as well. Thus, they connect the bank and the team, so they click on the ad, and then through the one or two clicks, they can open up an account and have that card delivered in the mail. Geo-fencing provides a way to find an audience in an area that allows you to deliver ads on mobile and also computers, but you're trying to just find a location and deliver ads at the right time and right place.

Geo-fencing is highly targeted. Beware of trying to mass target with geo because you'll get too many people in the message. Target your market and audience as precisely as possible.

You can do talking heads where they actually talk to the consumer. If they were near a bank, it would pop up, and they would see a video and welcome you to the location. You can create personal-ish connections with geo-fencing. It's using technology with location-based marketing to find a heat map or hot leads. And again, it's kind of like the new print. The coolest part of that is you can click through to a conversion, which doesn't occur in print marketing.

Geo-conquesting, as previously mentioned, is like the next level of geo-fencing. It's called conquesting because, as you can guess, you're picking your competition. If you're a bank and there are six other banks in your market, you can circle their banks and drop ads on them.

Why is that important? People only go into banks for three reasons: to open an account, close an account, or make a transaction. Two of those are in your favor. If they're going to open an account and you get an ad in front of them that has a better deal, they may leave and go open an account at your bank. You gave them an offer in the right place. If they're closing an account, they're going to need a new bank. You're giving them an offer at the right time. If they're making a transaction, you're just getting a brand impression. That's an example in financial services; it will work just as well in any business. For example, Foot Locker versus some other shoe company. If it's Foot Locker versus Champs or Academy Sports versus Dick's Sporting Goods, you then deliver a better deal.

If they're looking at their phone while they're shopping, they may see a better deal and click on it and purchase the product digitally while they're actually in your competitor's store. A great example of this was Burger King. They did a geo-conquesting campaign where they conquested all of the McDonald's in America. When you walked in, they sent you a message that conquested you and said, click here, and your Whopper is free if you leave the McDonald's. alistdaily.com/technology/burger-king-app-mcdonalds-whopper.

People were leaving McDonald's and going to buy Whoppers. It was one of the Cannes Award Festival winners. You could get a free Whopper, but only if you clicked on the ad while you were in McDonald's, and it showed from geo-tracking that you left McDonald's to go get your Whopper. It was a direct geo-conquest of an opponent, and it worked beautifully for Burger King.

SECTION ON SEO AND SEM

You have to know that search engine optimization and search engine marketing are very important today because they are like the subscription to your newspaper in the '50s or the eyeballs viewing your TV ads in the '60s. Who is viewing your product, and how are they getting there? When you write copy, or you're setting up for conversion and content, know how it's going to look when it's searched on Google, know how it's going to be placed on Google.

According to https://www.wordstream.com/meta-tags: Meta tags are snippets of text that describe a page's content. The meta tags don't appear on the page itself but only in the page's source code. Meta tags are essentially little content descriptors that help tell search engines what a web page is about.

The only difference between tags you can see (on a blog-post, say) and tags you can't see is the location: meta tags exist only in HTML, usually at the "head" of the page, and are only visible to search engines (and people who know where to look). The "meta" stands for "metadata," which is the kind of data these tags provide—data *about* the data on your page.

They're similar in that they're placed in the same rows, but one will have an ad beside it and one won't. Obviously, search engines control their own algorithms, so how you write copy is very important. If you don't know how to do that, get some help or learn. Even though the algorithm changes, you can still write to become effectively listed and make sure your listing is correct. It's like a modern phone book. You need to make sure your addresses are correct, your phone numbers are correct, your website's correct, your click-throughs are correct, the landing pages are correct, and that there are no broken links because the algorithms don't like broken links. Algorithms are set up in search engines for relevancy to the searcher aka your customer.

An example is *what time does the Super Bowl start?* A lot of people will search for what time the Super Bowl starts, and companies want their brand to come up in the search under what time the Super Bowl starts. But that's not what the consumer is trying to find.

It's a hack. Google figured that out, and now it has to be relevant to the Super Bowl, like an NFL website or a TV website. It can't be just any company that wants your eyeballs on their brand. Relevancy is important when it comes to search engine marketing and search engine optimization.

Looking at search engine optimization, it starts with that blank search line, that line on Google, Bing, Yahoo, YouTube, and so on. Marketers with relevancy can rise in the search listings. Research shows that the first listing gets 80% of the clicks, the second one gets 20%, and then the other ones get a fraction of that. Your listing and the relevancy of the search terms that found your listing are very important. Determine the analytics and algorithms for search engine optimization.

Google Ad Word Tools

Search engine marketing, specifically through Google AdWords, are ads that show up within the search engine results. There is a difference between search engine optimization (SEO) and search engine marketing (SEM), but they work well in tandem. Start with SEO because it's more affordable—focus on the way you write your copy and build that into your website or digital ads. Build it into SEM, which is how you create the marketing that lands on search engines.

Social media can be a great equalizer. If someone is interested in a brand or a product, they don't care if it's the big global company or if it's just a mom-and-pop selling shirts on the corner. If your social media presence connects, you must have a way for people to click through to get to your site, whether it be through

PayPal, Venmo, Zelle, Apple Pay, Google Pay, Square, etc., for them to convert.

With social media, it's important that you don't just use it as a branding process, but that you actually push toward a conversion at some point in the connectivity process. It can be a powerful tool. Allbirds shoes uses Facebook tremendously well. They show their shoes, they build short videos about them, then you click, and it takes you to the size and the color. One more click, and you've purchased your shoes. Other than entering a credit card, if you're doing it for the first time, they do a tremendous job, and they are not New Balance, Nike, or Adidas—they are a smaller shoe company competing with the mega brands.

Allbirds shoes does really well selling through social media, it's more people's faces as it's more intimate. If you can hit that emotion and show what someone wants at the right time, they'll click through to it. It also has reputational value because they can post about it—I like my shoes, I like this place to eat, I like this car. I like, I like, I like. You can increase your likes and followers. Social media can also convert on reputational marketing because people will look for things that get good reviews. Oh, my community of likes or followers likes that. They're like me, they're in my community so I'll buy it as well.

Let's look at Facebook. It, along with Instagram (which Facebook owns), are the most dominant social media platforms. It's the most recognized brand of social media in the US. We have Twitter, LinkedIn, Snapchat, TikTok, and whatever new one comes along tomorrow.

Facebook and Instagram for Marketing

An interesting sidebar: a lot of the millennials got off of Facebook when Instagram was becoming popular because they didn't want their parents to see their posts. Many moved to Instagram, thinking Facebook wasn't cool and didn't realize that Instagram was actually owned by Facebook.

Why are Facebook and Instagram important platforms to market on if that's a channel you want to use? First, it's probably less expensive compared to other marketing reach of the same nature. Secondly, if you can get a like, that's great. If you can get a share, even better because now you have organic reach. Your content is delivered by a customer or by a brand ambassador with more credibility. They share content that's now seen by consumers, so you can organically grow your reach without having to pay for it in the sense that you paid for the content, but you're not paying for that organic growth.

You can boost it. Boosting is buying views of your content. This is all part of the conversion because, if you don't have a big audience, likes, connects, or followers, you can boost your content to get views. If it's good and people like it, you can build an engaged audience. Facebook and Instagram do not allow you to place a conversion or a link in the photo, so go to the post under it and pin a post at the top that says "Donate to my nonprofit after you watch it," or "Buy this here," and give them a link to take them to the conversion site.

It doesn't have to be in the content because you can get creative and put it in the first comment or pin the top comment. Pinterest does really well at this because that's where the do-it-yourselfers go—the market that's looking for home goods and crafts. The sales part of it is pinning in those comments under it on where you can get what you're seeing in the picture or the photo or the content.

In social media, also think about who you can follow. You're on Facebook, and you have 30,000 followers. Follow them back, especially if they can be influential to you. They might post about you, or they might see that you followed them and engage in the future. It depends on your brand and what your brand message and style is, but if it's important to be connected to that consumer, it might be important that the consumer's connected to you as well.

Now you can also add your brand personality to it. A great example is Kentucky Fried Chicken. KFC only follows 11 people on social media, yet they have over three million followers. Do you know who they are? KFC follows 11 people because they have 11 herbs and spices. They follow the five Spice Girls and six random guys named Herb. By doing this, they've created a comical joke on social media with their followers. They've created brand humor, and the people who follow them also love their tone and snarkiness on social media.

In social media, the ROI or the conversion can be different from just making a sale. It can be building an audience, creating a brand following, building a community, increasing brand awareness, or receiving organic content growth. It can be placing content throughout social media channels to get awareness and to build reputational goodwill. It might be to build a list, have people opt in, then connect with them later. As every business wants to build their bottom line and make money, there has to be the start of a connection to get them to conversion. That can be a different ROI with social media than just the point of getting a credit card or a click to a payment processor. It can be really building your community, building your brand, building your followers, building your ambassadors, and so on.

When you look at social media, it needs to be taken a little differently from traditional sales models. Social media is personal to people. They have a profile of themselves. They're placing stuff about them, their likes, the things they wish for, their day, and their interactions. This is great data for you to have as a marketer. You can look at crosstabs on Facebook and see the majority of your likes, what they like, etc. Do they like country music? Do they shop at Walmart or Target? You could buy billboards on the way to Target, knowing that your customers travel there. There are many ways to use social media to partner with traditional media. That may be a way of using social media for conversion that's not a click to a credit card; it might be creating a database of things that your customers like or creating a survey that they take that builds a profile.

Without getting into campaigning claims like all the controversy surrounding Facebook, let's review the process. Building a survey that creates profiles of your customers is a way to glean data on how you can obtain the right wording for search engine optimization. What are they looking for when they're looking for a car or a bank? What benefits are they asking about with your product? Look at cross tabs of their likes. Do all of your likes also like Wendy's? Can you partner with Wendy's for a discount or a coupon? If you're a bank, can you partner with a car dealership and see that your customers really like this car dealership and your bank, and you have a lot of shared likes in the crosstabs? Could you partner up because you know that your customers are at the same place?

There's a lot of data that can be pulled from "likes" that creates a conversion that might not be in the social media channel, but in the big picture, can be a great conversion opportunity for brands. There are also mistakes that marketers often make and then wonder why they're not getting the conversion, the click-through, or whatever their ROI goal was for their campaign for the content they're delivering. Often, it's because they post it one time and think, *Well, I put something out there; why is everyone not liking it?* You have to be repetitive. It's just like in the traditional media of TV, where many studies say it takes 27 viewings of a commercial for anyone to recall it unless the commercial was something completely different and instantly memorable, which doesn't typically happen.

Imagine you post on social media, and every two seconds, there's a new post as you scroll through. You have to build the content to find itself in the feed. It might be a video today, audio a little bit later, a different part of the video, a shorter version of it. Then, all of a sudden, it's an article about your product that matches the video, and you're sending it two, three times a day or two, three times a week—whatever you think the right touch is for your brand. That's a mistake some make, is they're just *there* all the time. People will view that brand as being too much and not want to follow them anymore. Or you're never there, and then all of a sudden you show up, and you're thinking,

Well, I'm here. No one knows to follow or like you because they don't know about you.

Metaphorically, social media, especially Facebook, is like a dinner party, and you're invited to this party. Do you talk too much and annoy people? Do you not talk at all, and you're the weird quiet person in the corner, and then you say something dramatic, and people are like, "Whoa, don't do that." Think of a happy medium. You listen, and you talk a little bit, and you tell great stories, and you listen to people's stories, and you comment positively on their stories, or negatively if that's what you need to do. It's a digital party, and you're there. The content you put out should be interesting, the content you receive should be interesting, and how you interact should be interesting.

Again, if you're quiet, and then just say something dramatic, it will seem odd. If you talk all the time and never listen, react, or interact, then you're just the self-absorbed narcissist and no one wants to be your friend. You can find success in social media by finding the balance between how much you interact and not interact, and when to interact and when not to interact. If you get a negative response, you don't want to stir it up with a back and forth that gets eyeballs on it and becomes a negative brand.

It's unfortunate because you want to treat all customers the same, but if someone has three followers, and they're cussing you out on social media, just step back and monitor it. Think about blocking them. If not, monitor the situation. If someone has 100,000 followers, reach out directly to them and say, "Hey, we need to fix this issue." It's sad to say you don't look at everybody the same, but the fact is everyone doesn't have the same impact on your brand. Be very cognizant of who your followers are and what impact they have, as well as their influence. They might not be an influencer in the traditional sense of an Instagram model hawking some type of clothing, but they might be very influential in their community. By posting something negative, you need to reach out quickly and figure out how to solve their problem.

Social media is like brand proofing for you. It's proof of your success in connecting with your audience, and the way they interact with you shows that you have proof of a good brand. If you're good at it, you could ask them for a review. Don't be afraid to ask for a good review, a like, or a share. We're talking about conversion here; you're asking for the business. If your ROI is growing a brand, building an audience, and getting likes, then why not ask for it? Ask for the like if your conversion is a like. If your conversion is a share, ask for it. Say, "Please review my product." That way, you also get data back. What have you done wrong that you aren't aware of? What are the opportunities you're missing or don't see?

Interacting on social media and asking for proof of your brand, proof of your concept, is free polling or free shopping for your brand. Social media can be used in so many ways. When you think of social media and conversion, don't just think about dollars.

We care about dollars, and it's very important. Let's not discount that the bottom line is still going to be the most important metric you have with your management team. But getting to that bottom line might not be a direct sale or direct click to checkout; it might be building a community, building shares or likes to get to a better conversion in the long game.

Every company should have online sales abilities. Every business in today's marketing must have the ability to convert online and have an online account opening system or apparatus to convert a customer. Why not show up to get your oil changed and have it already paid for rather than just dropping your car off and waiting in line to pay? Starbucks does this with their app where you can prepay and pre-order. You've already converted, and it causes less time for the barista and less time for you. Their online account process is really quick, and it's all done through their app.

Sam's Club allows you to walk in with your phone and use it as a barcode reader and walk up to the front and have already paid. Companies do this from location-based as well as geo-based, but if your company does not have a way to convert over phone or over a digital apparatus, you need to investigate that first before you start marketing content and connection. If you get the customer there and they can't convert, why did you do the first two Cs (content and connection) anyway?

Time is the ultimate commodity because everyone has the same amount. Rich or poor, you have the same number of hours in the day and the same number of days in the year. How can we save more time? You can purchase online or in brick-and-mortar stores. You can buy your groceries in the store or have them delivered to your house, but saving the hour you'd have to go in and shop by having things delivered makes a huge difference. And then, if you're one of the companies that does it well, market that experience: "You don't even have to go in anymore; we'll deliver to you." Uber Eats will pick it up. You can pre-order at Starbucks, then your order is saved so you don't ever have to type it in again. You just click *Same*, and it repeats every day if you have the same drink or the same meal.

By building a CRM or using an MCIF that does this through conversion, you can not only save their time, but you can also save their preferences. And you know what? That builds brand loyalty: "They know who I am as a person. They know what I want. I'm not going anywhere else because they get me."

A/B testing is very important in conversion. A/B testing is taking one thing and calling it A and an alternate setup and calling it B and running them together to see which one is the most effective. An A/B test might be placing a red *Buy Now* button on one version of your page and a blue *Buy Now* button on another version, then tracking the number of visits to see which one gets the most clicks.

It can work for anything. If it's a Facebook ad, does color matter when placing a link in it versus a button? What about the audience it's delivered to as you build a Facebook-targeted campaign? If it's sent to 20- to 25-year-old-college females in the Southeast, does it work best if it has pink or blue colors? Test colors, layout and copy and then adopt the best test with your data to make a more successful conversion rate.

With A/B tests, you realize the most subtle changes can change your conversion. A color, a word, the font, kerning, logo placement—anything at all—can change the ability for that person to get there. The repetition of the button, the click-through link, the call-out for the sale, the photograph, the image and what's in it, how it relates to that person—it can all make a difference to your market, to your ability to convert. Is it a picture of a family or an individual? Is it a picture of a certain life genre? Is it a picture of a certain lifestyle? Is it a product picture? Is it a cartoon or animation versus a real person?

In conversion, when you're looking at your strategy of getting someone to the point of sale or to the point of whatever your conversion is, microsites are a great way to send them directly to what they're looking to find. A microsite is just a website, but it's built on a specific communication point versus a full home page. It's micro-focused. "Buy this jacket," for example. You don't want to send them to the apparel site where they have to look through shoes, hats, and shirts. You send them directly to a microsite that converts them to buy that jacket because, if they're contemplating whether or not to buy your product and you send them to another product, you might confuse them and lose the customer because they get distracted. You lose that moment when they're about to make the decision.

The microsite is a good way of getting people specifically what they need, and they're inexpensive to build vs an entire site or lost chance a conversion (no more next time). You don't have to build a full site with content or build out a communication plan, connectivity, call center, updates, etc. It's just a small site, a single page. Content-wise, it can even be completely mobile, built specifically for the mobile experience. Microsites are very important to your conversion process because you can specifically land the consumer on where you want them to go and where they're expecting to buy the product.

Speaking of mobile, it's hard to imagine that a company today would not have a mobile-friendly website. But they're out there. Look around, you probably bump into one about every three or four sites you visit. If your site isn't mobile-optimized, if you have to pinch and grab and drag and move around and slide, you lose another consumer because they're used to being able to have a good experience for the brands that do it well, and you're competing against them. It's not just your industry, it's all brands that do mobile. You must have a mobile-optimized site where there's no pinching, dragging, moving around, or turning the phone sideways to get the full site up. It needs to adjust for mobile so you can make the conversion process easier and have a better experience for your customer.

In addition to being mobile-optimized, you must have a mobile strategy. Does that involve geo? Yes. Does that involve geo-conquesting? Yes. Does that involve content and how it's delivered and social media? Because all that is part of a mobile strategy, and it's now different for every business. How do you get people to find your restaurant on their phone? It might be your reputation, it might be Yelp, or your stars or ranking on various restaurant reviews. That may be your strategy. If you're trying to click to purchase, your strategy might be how you place ads that are mobile-friendly and what your process is to have them click through to make the final purchase. Then, how do you build content to remind them of the product on mobile? There are many types of mobile strategies, but you need to have at least one.

Beyond having a mobile strategy, you should also have a drip process strategy, which is content touchpoints at different times for your brand. That could be sending an email to your email subscription list but knowing that those same people are on Facebook, so what content are you putting on Facebook that matches that email list? Oh, and by the way, you're geo-fencing them because they're shopping in a certain area, so you're putting the same messaging there. This is all about taking a holistic approach to your marketing and getting different touchpoints to be in front of your client.

The drip campaign is putting them in your MCIF system and sending six emails this month, or six emails this year, whatever you're comfortable with, and touching them six times digitally. Oh, and they've gone in our location four or five times, and we know that they've looked at this ad or they've looked at this website a few times. And by doing that, you build touchpoints for your customers, and you can drip content to them that connects and, eventually, creates a conversion.

For conversion, we've talked about social media and digital, we've talked a lot about online purchasing processes and having a mobile strategy. Let's not forget more traditional marketing. Many people prefer a tactile experience. They want to feel the clothing before they buy it. They want to experience a restaurant before they place their order. There's still an end game to the consumer consuming a product, and a lot of that has to have a physical impact or physical experience versus just a digital experience. Let's not forget that while we're talking about shiny, new, and cool, there is still the physical experience that matters.

If someone has a poor experience, there's no next time. That next time now might be a bad review, or it might be ranting about you on social media. So you might be great on digital, but if the personal experience is bad, you might be creating a bad brand experience at the same time. Traditional, mobile, and digital now have the same brand quality feel because, again, it can impact you just as much tangibly as it does virtually.

TACTICAL TAKEAWAYS

The Great Eight of Conversion

1. **Test, test, test.** We cannot talk enough about how important it is to run your campaigns through A/B testing, your conversion testing, where nodules and buttons and other apparatus to get conversion are on a site or on your digital strategy or even in a physical location. Where's the cash register placed? Where's the menu placed? Where's the point of sale? Test, test, and test again.

2. **Have a digital conversion platform for mobile and desktop.** It's one thing to have a digital platform; it's another for it not to be optimized for mobile. If it's

built for mobile and they can't get to it or have it look properly on their desktop, you may lose the conversion.

3. **Have a conversion that works with all browsers.** Yes, people still use Internet Explorer. About 3% of the marketplace in corporate America still use Internet Explorer, according to gs.statcounter.com statistics. Even though it might look good in Chrome, it must look good, and work, in most browsers. Build any sales conversion or web or content platform to work on all browsers that are readily available in the marketplace.

4. **Make it as simple as possible.** Remember the phrase, "If you're explaining, you're losing." If the consumer can't figure out how to put their credit card in, if it takes ten minutes to join a club and provide all your information, it will be a turnoff for the customer. Try to make it simple with as few clicks as possible and as quickly as possible because time is still the ultimate commodity in today's marketplace.

5. **Build for what people expect or what they are used to using.** Amazon has created a decent experience on the conversion platform. They have a cart, they save your credit card or payment method of choice, and it reduces the data entry process. Unfortunately for a lot of businesses, this has become the way consumers expect the conversion process to be for them. So they expect it to be easy to click through and not have to spend a lot of time doing data entry. They expect to be able to go straight to PayPal or straight to Apple Pay and pay for their conversion, so obviously build for the experience people expect.

6. **Landing pages must match the campaign.** This strikes to our point about microsites—don't advertise an item and then push the consumer to a homepage where they

get lost in all of your products. Build a microsite that takes them directly to what they're looking for with the ability to convert immediately. After the conversion, you may add in, "Do you want to join our club? Do you want a discount on this? Do you want to see more items that we have?" Do that after the initial emotional buy/purchase consideration process.

7. **Use your data.** Use your data to look at where people are visiting on your site, how they're bouncing in and around it. Use it to look at social media crosstabs. Use it to look at where people are physically entering your building and what the customer experience is when they visit a physical location. Heat map how they get there; look at the trail of how your customers arrive at your location. Look at the data around geo-fencing and how they're receiving your digital ads and their click-through rates.

8. **Know what you're trying to do to produce the KPIs and ROIs you need.** This might involve impressions, likes, shares, or reviews, so know what you're looking for when you start the campaign. As Stephen Covey said, "Begin with the end in mind." Begin knowing what you're going to measure and how you're going to measure it, so you can report properly when your conversion process is finished.

That's the great eight of conversion. By paying attention to the great eight, you will find more success in the conversion of your content.

The Hateful Eight of Conversion

1. **Not being able to convert off your content.** You can have beautiful advertising, awesome digital campaigns, and a great connection with your customer, but if you

can't get a click-through that collects money, you've failed in revenue collection. You have to be able to convert a customer into a sale at some point.

2. **Not being mobile-friendly.** We've harped on this throughout, but if your campaign does not lead to a mobile-friendly experience and they're having to pinch, drag, resize, and try to type something in that overlays poorly, you will lose clicks.

3. **Forgetting the human connection.** Again, there is a human connection to all marketing, and if you think it's just digital, you will lose because there's still the physical impact of locations, dealerships, and restaurants where people want an experience. Digital may lead them to the experience or sale, but don't forget the human connection of conversion.

4. **Forgetting to ask for the business.** You might have a great ad, you might have a great digital campaign, you may have a great social campaign—but at the end of it, if you're not asking for the business or asking for the conversion, you will lose the ability to gain a ROI.

5. **Not being able to measure.** Television was and maybe still is the greatest marketing apparatus of all time, but it is really hard to measure. You might know the impressions, but it's hard to see an impact on the bottom line in the macro. Know how to measure and create the ability to measure, whether it be through CRM and MCIF systems or through direct mail and putting data against data to call out the conversions. Know how to measure and be able to measure your campaigns.

6. **Providing a poor conversion experience.** A poor conversion experience can kill a great marketing campaign. You may have the best content that gets the consumer

to a great connection, but if your conversion process is poorly mapped out, doesn't collect data properly, or is inefficient with timing, it creates a poor conversion experience that creates poor ROI.

7. **Follow up.** Just because you post something one time on social media or create one ad or place one print ad or one billboard, it doesn't mean it's going to work or that people will see it. You must take a holistic marketing approach, especially when you get to the point of conversion. How do you collect the data, especially if it's digitally of the drop-offs and breakage in there? You need to have a plan to revisit via email or digital, or even in-person or a phone call or text. How do you revisit the breakage in your conversion process? Follow-up can be important to get the sale that you missed the first time. Always have a plan to follow up on breakage and repetition in your marketing to get to the conversion point that might not have been reached the first time in your conversion process.

8. **No follow-up with those that know you.** Not realizing that your warmest markets are current clients and referrals. The most cost-effective marketing is to your current client base because they are already aware of your brand and might even be fans of it. When you're looking at campaigns, especially to convert, don't forget your current clients. New clients are always fun and exciting, but current client expansion often has better results. So don't forget about your current clients when looking at the conversion process.

CHAPTER 4
THE FOURTH C: CAMPAIGNS

"Comfort is the ultimate addiction."

–Ronnie Doss

Ronnie Doss is a personal and business coach, and he starts off many of his presentations with that quote. That's a good intro for campaigns because people get comfortable, and they don't want to take a risk. They want to do the same thing over and over again because it worked in the past. There is a graveyard of companies that would not take risks, were comfortable with what they were doing, and it became their addiction. There are many industries littered with disruption because people became too addicted to the comfort of their industry.

I'm in banking. it seems we're disrupted every day from latest FinTech idea, a new app that exchanges money differently from traditional banking, cryptocurrencies, and technologies that distract and pull away from the traditional means of banking and moving money. The marketplace changes, and when you get addicted to the comfort of your marketing, you don't do things differently. You might still be doing traditional advertising more than you need to or you might be doing too much in social because you've gotten comfortable with that as a newer company, and you don't realize getting out of your comfort zone may actually help you.

Thinking outside of your comfort zone or your traditional target may introduce you to a new market. It may introduce you to a whole new group of consumers you don't know. Comfort is something that holds us back in marketing. While we should take calculated risks, don't go out and blow up your marketing plan and come back with a new plan that changes your business if you're already successful. But you must not be addicted to comfort. That's why we're moving on to the fourth Cs—campaigns—which uses the three Cs to get there and pull together our campaigns.

CASE STUDY: RALPH LAUREN

We talked about Tommy Hilfiger earlier, but one of his competitors, Ralph Lauren, has also been somewhat of a disruptor in the way he originally marketed his retail product. When he walked into Bloomingdale's or Nordstrom's or another retailer in New York, he saw that they didn't display his clothing the way he wanted. That's an experience for the consumer. Instead of complaining or worrying about it, he just went and built his own stores. By building his own stores, he could adjust his marketing and experience the way he wanted it. Again, marketing is not just digital, it's customer experience. He wanted the experience to be about Ralph Lauren and Polo, not just the experience they had in another retailer with him being in a certain area of the store.

Then, he thought, *Why do I just have to have the affluent prep market? I can go after an urban market.* He created Polo Sport and a whole line of bigger brand, bigger logoed items that fit the hip hop and athletic industry for the urban fashionista versus the traditional Polo. He changed his apparel, but he didn't change it to get rid of one. He added to increase market share. I think that's because he wasn't comfortable. He said, "I have this area, let's go to this area. I have this experience that people should have, and they're not getting it here." It's all brand marketing. We look at the Tommy Hilfigers, who didn't make an advertisement like the Ralph Laurens, the Perry Ellis's, and the Calvin Kleins. We look at Ralph Lauren, who created his own experience that was Americana Prep *and* Americana Urban to hit two markets. It probably wasn't a particularly comfortable process, and it wasn't cheap, but in the end, it created a brand that has stood the test of time and is one of the strongest, most-recognized fashion brands in the world.

In marketing campaigns with today's channels of delivery, you can own your own content, you can own your own audience, and you can own your own likes, followers, and fans. In the past, you were beholden to big media. There's nothing wrong with traditional big media, but you are beholden to them for distribution. You could get on five television stations, big news conglomerates for newspapers, and multimedia publishers.

But now with content studios and looking at it yourself as a media company versus a widget company, car company, brewery, clothing manufacturer, or whatever your product happens to be, you can own your content, you can own the process, and you can even own the conversion. You need to have partners to make the financial transaction, but the experience can be owned by yourself.

Much like some of the brands we've talked about in this book, they've taken campaigns upon themselves and become their own delivery apparatus. You can, too. Look at your marketing and say, "Can we get on social and make our own content? Can we create our own without having television commercials or the news media to tell our story? Can we tell our own story? Can we create our own fans that back up our story? Then create a brand reputation, and then we go about our day and look at conversion and how we make this into money?"

Campaigns are the fourth C. It's taking the three—content, connection, and conversion—and putting them together into tactical practice. Your marketing needs to start with content because content is information, and content marketing is delivering information to an audience. Your content might include video, print, and experience. What is that content, and how does it connect? It does this in two ways. That's the emotional tie to the brand, and that's also the tactical delivery of connection. Social, digital, traditional, personal experience—you've got that.

Then there's conversion. How do you make the content connect and then convert SEO, web, OAO, and everything we've talked about in the previous chapters? Finally, you put the three together to create campaigns, and the campaigns are the delivery of your marketing brand message.

When you want to begin your campaign, it starts around ideas. Now, ideas are nothing more than what they are. They're ideas. If you can't convert them, if you can't execute on them, they're useless. Everyone has ideas. Every consumer of your company probably has an idea about what they think you should do. There's no shortage of ideas in marketing; ask any employee at your company. They probably have a marketing idea. Finding the right idea to turn it into content that will eventually connect is where you win in brand marketing. It all starts with an idea, but that idea has to be useful and be able to connect and execute. When you start with an idea, look at how it becomes content and look at how it meets the other Cs going forward.

In campaigns, the idea for the campaign can be different from the product, it can be different from the value, and it can be different from the benefit. When you're mapping out ideas, when you go to the whiteboard, when you're brainstorming for your ideas, know that you don't have to start with a conversion in mind. You'll have to get there, but look at all your ideas and formulate how it's going to be content and recognize that there's not just one idea for a product or one idea for a campaign.

If you're a marketer looking at your campaign and trying to start off with your ideas and your concepts for content, this is where you get to create your brand personality. That brand personality can be fun. You can be like KFC's or Wendy's snarky social media brand. Or you can be serious. You can be Volvo, and it's all about safety. Or at least the perception of it. An example of the power of great branding and communication can be found in the book *Hey, Whipple, Squeeze This: A Guide to Creating Great Ads*, where Luke Sullivan writes the following about Volvo:

In every speech I've ever given, anywhere around the world, when I ask audiences, "What does Volvo stand for?" I hear the same answer every time: "Safety." Audiences in Berlin, Reykjavik, Helsinki, Copenhagen, New York City *all* give the same answer. The money Volvo has spent on branding has paid off handsomely. Volvo has successfully spot-welded that one adjective to their marquee. And here's the interesting bit: In the past couple of years, Volvo hasn't even made it onto the top 10 list of safest cars on the market. So here's a brand that, having successfully paired its logo to one adjective, rides the benefit of this simple positioning in customers' minds long after its products no longer even merit the distinction. Such is the power of simplicity.

Volvo's simplicity in messaging lead to a connection with its audience of being the safe car. What can it be for your brand? It can be more connectivity. It can be with phone carriers and how you connect with your family and share those great moments. It can be the military and the emotions of that soldier coming home to their family. When you're looking for content ideas, look at emotion.

But also look at the brand personality you want to deliver to your audience. Are you fun? Are you cool? Are you informational? Are you wise? Are you silly? Are you the one who's not too serious, or are you very serious because you sell life insurance? What is your brand personality? Put that into your content. Because if you're authentic, people will feel it. And when it's real, there'll be a fan.

A great example of campaign marketing during the writing of this book is Disney Plus. When they had just launched their new streaming app, there was a lot of hype around it because they had bought *Star Wars* and Marvel, along with Pixar and National Geographic, plus all the original Disney movies. You had all these great, timeless content pieces that were all going to be owned by Disney and released as a streaming app. But Disney is not a mobile delivery company; it's an entertainment and experience company. It has some of the most loyal and raving fans of any brand. One of the most popular brands in the world, actually. In doing that, they built tremendous hype and campaign about Disney Plus. But they decided they needed a partner to deliver their product, so they teamed up with Verizon to help them with their campaigns and their connection.

When you look at your campaign and how it will be delivered, make sure you have the right partners because there will be parts you can't do yourself. There are good and bad aspects of Disney Plus. The good part is they had millions of subscribers on day one. Any company would kill to have their subscriptions and brand loyalty. The downside of this is they were too successful in their marketing, in their hype, and they actually had problems with server space to get apps downloaded as well as streaming. Branding was so successful in their partnership, and they were so successful in their campaign, that it was looked at as they were "just over the top in subscribing right out of the gate."

When building a campaign, especially a modern campaign, there are many more options than there used to be. Can you put the product in a show? When campaigns used to be built around commercials, they didn't have the same eyeballs or impact they used to, but people still watch certain shows and live sporting events. That's why the Super Bowl is so popular. That's why college sports are so popular.

Do you buy television commercials in the big games, or do you look at product placement during the game? If it's MLS, can you get your name on the jersey? If it's NASCAR, do you have your name on a car? If it's tennis, do you have your name on the headband a tennis player is wearing? If it's football, do you have it on the coach's headset? Do you have it on the backdrop of the goalpost? Do you have it on the basket in basketball? Can you find a way beyond sports to place your brand within a show or a television event? When you look at campaigns, think creatively and not just think, "Well, we need to buy commercials." That's an old mindset.

You might be able to get it within the show, but could you place it in the movie? If you watch a modern James Bond movie, it is nothing but product placement.

Heineken, Aston Martin, Omega watches, and so on. It's a beer, it's a car, it's a watch, or it's a suit. It's product placement throughout the entire movie. Because you're distracted, you don't look at it as a commercial. But you're actually watching one big commercial because James Bond is an attempt at a luxury lifestyle brand product placement. Even though he's a womanizer and a licensed killer, he is still a great brand apparatus for that genre and the audience that loves the action fantasy with its exotic locations.

CASE STUDY: POPEYES CHICKEN

Popeyes Chicken released a new chicken sandwich. Why would a chicken sandwich go viral and be popular? It's because they did a great job of cultivating a Twitter following that promoted it. They paid NFL players to wear Popeyes Chicken cleats on the rollout of their new chicken sandwich. But here was the biggest gain of their campaign: they built it around competition weakness. The *Art of War* by Sun Tzu talks about attacking your opponent from his weakest point. Chick-fil-A is their biggest competitor. Guess what? Chick-fil-A is not open on Sundays. When did Popeyes release their chicken sandwich? On a Sunday. They had no competitor on Sunday, so no one would see the other chicken sandwich. They took advantage of Chick-fil-A's brand placement. Now, Chick-fil-A's brand is to be closed on Sunday because of their values. And that's their choice. But Popeyes took advantage to start delivery of their brand on Sunday, which is *their* choice: https://www.thrillist.com/news/nation/popeyes-chicken-sandwich-back-november-2019.

Look at your brand and decide what your personality is and how you will reach your audience and take advantage of opportunities to wedge into consumer preferences.

When are building your campaign, don't be afraid of being competitive or taking on your competition. After all, it is a competition for business. If you're afraid of taking on the competition, you'll just be in the middle. You have to find a way to look at others' weaknesses as your advantages. Look at your advantages versus your competition. Are you better on price? Are you better on location? Are you better on content? There's this story of a donut company and a pie company that were across the street from each other. They went back and forth on their billboards and bought each other's billboards on top of their locations. It's an interesting story about how they went back and forth with messages: https://www.wsj.com/articles/SB1000142405297020 47554045781030639645009222.

While it looks snarky and competitive, it just grew their brand awareness to where everyone wanted to see what would happen the next time they changed their billboards. You have these great competitions and competitors against each other, but yet, they both win.

In American business culture, we like to see healthy competition. There are winners and losers whether we want to admit it or not. Don't be afraid to build a campaign around acknowledging your competition or taking on your competition or looking at your weaknesses and your advantages that you have against your competition.

You must test and track your campaigns. Just throwing out content, throwing out a sales campaign, and not tracking it, is a recipe for failure from not being able to adjust and make it better. When you plan your content, make it trackable at some level. Again, know what your KPIs are for your marketing initiatives. Is it conversions? Is it dollars and sales? Is it building an audience? Is it cross-referencing and building an audience you can share with another client-partner?

Measuring success in a campaign can come in many different ways. When you start out building content, have a team build ways to measure that content. In other words, what is the ultimate goal of this campaign? Is it to gain attention? Because, if that's so, it's impressions. Is it money? If that's so, it's the benefit to value to product. Is it followers and likes? Is it content? Is it partnering with an influencer? Determine what you want it to be in the beginning and then have that as part of your overall strategy in your campaign.

When looking at campaigns, they should be the all-encompassing delivery of your content, your connection, and your conversion. When thinking of the campaigns, you might think that's just part of marketing, but it's the delivery of what you're trying to do. The campaign has to be the cornerstone of all those other things you want to deliver. The other three Cs of content, connection, and conversion with campaigns as the wrapper around all the "stuff" you're doing. When you start out, always look at how you will build the campaign. What are you going to do within it? What are the goals you wish to achieve?

In campaigns, timing is also very important. People will run campaigns, and they'll end them wondering why they should end a successful campaign. Most campaigns have a shelf life, but many are so good that they do become evergreen brand messaging.

CASE STUDY: CHICK-FIL-A COWS

A great example would be the Chick-fil-A cows. A 1995 billboard message of *Eat More Chicken* became their entire brand. What a creative way to deliver a brand message that's innocent and fun that appeals to adults and children alike. The cows don't want you to eat them because they're hamburgers! Who knew? They're up against hamburger restaurants like McDonald's, Burger King, and Wendy's, and they're trying to get you to eat chicken. Simple yet creative messaging. They created a cow mascot that has a call to action: eat more chicken. The way they delivered it created differentiation and connected to their audience. You can read more about this story here: https://www.adweek.com/brand-marketing/chicken-beef-untold-story-chick-fil-cow-campaign-171834/.

When you look at campaigns, they have life cycles. In politics, they have an election cycle, and there's an ending date. If you have a sale, you have a date that the sale will end. But if you find a niche campaign or brand message that resonates, make it endure. Chick-fil-A is a great example because that cow campaign has now endured for nearly 25 years. It's probably not going anywhere anytime soon. Dos Equis beer had one as well with the "most interesting man in the world." They tried to take him away, and the fans wanted him back because it was such an iconic campaign. If you find something that resonates with meme culture, you may want to reassess the life of any campaign.

There are two timings in a campaign. There's the timing of the calendar, and there's the timing of the content interest in the campaign. Great marketers will know how to use both of those to their advantage.

As a child, I was a big fan of books where you chose your own adventure. When you read the books, they will say things like, "If you would have shot the monster, turn to page 27. If you would have run away, turn to page 36. If you go for help from the village, turn to page 47." Or something of that nature. These action books let you choose your adventure.

In a similar fashion, I'm going to offer help as you choose your next campaign. Since technology allows us to be interactive, why not use this book as a living resource? If you have any questions or would like help, text me at **662-205-6288** or email me at **campaignmarketinghelp@gmail.com**. I'd be flattered - and I'm flattered that you read this far!

You can visit my site, www.johnoxford.com, and download a campaign outline or a campaign plan to fill in the blanks and help direct your way to be successful with the four Cs. At this point in the book, you can now choose to build your own campaign with what you've just read and learned.

QUESTIONS TO ANSWER FOR YOUR CAMPAIGNS

1. **Start with content.** What does your content need to be? What is your brand message going to be? What do you want your brand personality to be? Think through how you want your brand to be thought about in the public space.

2. **What is it you're trying to accomplish?** Is it likes? Followers? Conversions? Sales? Is it just dollars, or is it building a community of fans, influencers, or ambassadors? What are you trying to accomplish?

What are your goals, and how are you going to measure them? Write down how you're going to measure these goals.

Also, how can you test them? How are you going to test the colors, the feel, the messaging, and the target?

Think about how you're going to test and measure your campaign.

How are you going to deploy your campaign and execution?

What is your target?

What mediums are you going to use for delivery? Is it social? Is it traditional? Is it digital? Is it television, print, billboard, radio, referral, door-to-door, text, direct mail, phone calls?

How will you tell it if it is successful? What are your plans to adjust?

What's your budget? How can you shift during the campaign?

As you look through all of these, think about how the four Cs impact your marketing. How does your content work in this space? Are you using it for every medium possible? Are you producing many different pieces of content to match the channels and the audiences you want to receive your content? Is it connecting with them? Is it working on emotion, empathy, humor, education, smartness, awareness? How is it connecting with your consumer, and then how will it convert? Does it convert through clicks? Through a credit card? Does it use a payment system? How will it convert?

Decide your KPIs and how to measure them. We've repeated this a few times throughout the book, but they are different for every campaign. Is it dollars? Clicks? Likes? Then decide how you're going to measure it and figure that out as you're building your content. There's the old saying, "We're building the plane as we're flying it."

Adjust content and campaigns where you see there's weakness and then keep repeating if it's successful. Look at all your campaigns and say, "This was really good. If we did this, would it be just that much more successful?" Always test and always adjust as you need to be more successful.

TACTICAL TAKEAWAYS

The Great Eight (or Five) of Campaigns

Mark Penn, chairman and CEO of multi-agency holding company, MDC, has five things he thinks should be in every campaign. While borrowing from Mark, but giving him credit, I'm going to talk about these, and these will be our great eight but cut down to five for brevity.

1. **Every campaign needs some form of a slogan.** It needs some form of brand messaging. It can't just be, "Here's a video, here's a print ad, here's a commercial." It has to have some slogan about what you're supposed to do with this item you're selling. He says a slogan is always good, so start with some slogan or message.

2. **There has to be a bio of the product.** What is it? Why do I need it? What's the benefit?

3. **Who are you targeting with your campaign and what are you trying to accomplish with the target?** Who is

your audience? Is it niche? Is it the under-banked? The over-banked? Is it growing wallet share? Is it creating wallet share? Is it value? Is it luxury? What is your target audience and how can you hit them?

Take note: If you change your target during a campaign, it doesn't mean you necessarily have to change your campaign. You might find during testing that your target is different than you thought, and their campaign should have been directed toward a different target. That only means you discovered a different target. You might have thought it was a luxury brand when it's more of a value brand. Or you might have thought of it as a lower-value brand, while it's actually a luxury brand. You don't know until you test, and then you start targeting and realize, "Oh, this group is looking at our product and not the group we anticipated." You might not course-correct the campaign; you might course-correct the target of your next campaign.

If you're testing and you see it, changing the course for better results makes you a better marketer. Politicians do it all the time. They look at a direction in the campaign, then shift to a different issue because it becomes more popular, or they'll create popularity for an issue that takes away from a weakness on another issue. Target and message course-correction is vital to your campaign; I always look for chances to make it better because it can never be perfect.

4. **What are the issues or value of your campaign?** What's the value you're bringing to the consumer, and how are you making the consumer aware of the value?

5. **What is your edge against the competition?** You need to have a difference, or you wouldn't be there. What differentiates you from your competition? What is your

edge, and how do you deliver that edge and a brand message to your endgame consumer in a campaign?

Hateful Eight of Campaigns

1. **No quality or weak content.** When you're looking at your campaign, make sure you have quality content in two different ways: production and delivery.

2. **No message.** You need to have a clear message that your consumer "gets." Earlier, we talked about political messaging and slogans in your political campaigns. They endure, and you remember them because they were well done, and they hit the electorate at the right time and place in the nation's narrative. Make sure you have a message that resonates and is memorable.

3. **No connection.** You might have beautiful content, but it must also connect. You might have really amazing advertisements, but they don't connect with an audience because you've just put a lot of dollars behind them banking on repetition. Remember, people still make the purchase on emotion. If you can't connect, you need to revamp your campaign. It must connect with your audience to be successful.

4. **Being unable to convert.** You can't convert if you don't have the ability to transact, have them like, you send them to the wrong website, they Google your location, and it has a bad address, or you haven't cleaned up your SEO. They will go to the wrong place, or you send them to a competitor by accident. You've eliminated your ability to convert.

5. **Too similar.** Don't do a "light" campaign just like somebody else. It's very tempting to do, especially in commoditized businesses. We look at the competition and think, "Well, they're doing this." I can't tell you how

many times in our business other associates in the field will send us an ad from a competitor and say, "Well, look at what they're doing." You do need to be aware of what your competition is doing, but don't copy them.

In your campaigns, it is important to research what your competition is doing. After all, they may be finding niches in the market that would be advantageous for you, and you may actually serve the audience better than they do. Research is very important, whether you do it yourself or hire a company. It's also important so you don't accidentally copy. Many industries think the same way and hire many of the same people. You might, by circumstance or just by accident, do the same thing as another competitor just because you use many of the same people in your industry. Look at your competition and research them but do it also so you don't accidentally stumble on doing the same thing someone else is doing right. Never underestimate good opposition or competitive research.

6. **Not memorable or not enough resources to make it known.** Your campaigns need to be memorable, and it's probably the hardest thing to do in a campaign because who knows what's going to be memorable? It may come down to subjectivity. Although subjective, try to make it memorable, especially on the content side, so it connects. However, sometimes brands can be so repetitive that they create artifice memory of their campaigns. Capital One Cafe is an excellent example because their advertising is not what I would describe as super memorable from a creative perspective. However, they put so many resources behind it that it became a well-known and recalled message for their brand. For repetition and delivery, it was very memorable. When you look at your resources, many big brands may not be as memorable

with their content messaging, but by playing it repetitively with a lot of resources, they can make it memorable on a sign.

7. **Paralysis by analysis.** When you're building your campaign, don't get caught on the numbers so much that you can't make anything creative. Many a squirrel lies dead in the middle of the road from indecision. There's the right and left brain of every campaign. How are we going to hit the numbers? How are we going to grab attention? How are we going to make our KPIs and our ROI? How are we going to hit an emotional benefit with our consumers? Don't fall into paralysis because you're trying to analyze everything. Eventually, you have to execute, and you have to make a decision. I think that's a bigger picture in corporate America. You read a lot of business books, and they talk about just needing someone to make a decision. Some great marketing and business advice can be taken from General Patton when he famously said, "A good plan, violently executed now, is better than a perfect plan next week."

Timing is very important. It's important to be first to market if you can. There's also second-to-market companies that look at the first-to-markets and then try to improve on their offer. What's your brand message on that? Are you the leading edge of the spear, or are you the one who waits and looks at what happens because you're a little more conservative? Or you realized you didn't do it as well as the first time, but you created a better product to backfill the weaknesses in that opening product. Are you the front-runner, or are you the "make it better" brand? Be prepared and plan your timing well because you don't want to miss your window.

8. **No ROI.** Consider that sometimes a direct ROI is difficult to measure. Come up with a way of measuring your

content, measuring your connection, and measuring conversion. At the end of the campaign, you'll have an ROI that should show some success in your plan, even if it's not a hard dollar return.

Campaigns are the delivery vehicle of the first three Cs, and they're how you tactically deliver your marketing plan. As we move past the traditional four Ps of the fifties and into the four Cs of the new millennium of marketing (and even into the third decade of it), the old ways are dying quickly. As you've read through this book, you might think, "Okay, I understand content. I understand connection. I understand conversion. Now, I have to build my own campaign." But be aware that no campaign is ever perfect; there are mistakes every time you build one.

Although we marketers hate to admit it, sometimes campaigns fail. But you learn from the failures. Learn from your mistakes and your successes. You're always reviewing. Know that campaigns are tricky. They are complex, but when you do them right, they will help you be successful in executing the other three Cs.

Chapter 5
Using the Four Cs

While most of the book and the four Cs—content, connection, conversion, and campaigns—is written and built for corporate marketers and marketing students, this is not just a book about corporate marketing. If you're an individual who has your own business, whether it's trying to be a speaker or a conference persona, or whether it's trying to sell your own product, or be an entrepreneur or a startup, the four Cs are relevant to any marketing situation.

If you're trying to start a blog about your ideas, it's content. It's, how does it connect to your audience? And how do you convert your audience to be readers of your blog? Look through the four Cs and ask yourself, "How does this impact me individually?" As a salesperson, how are you connecting to tell your story and bring value? How are you converting people to be customers? If you own a restaurant, what's the content about the restaurant? Do you build connection with the food, the benefits, and the warmth of being there? And then, finally, how do you convert to get the customer there?

As you complete this book, the number one takeaway is simple: marketing is always changing. No longer can you look at the four Ps as the foundation of marketing; it's now the four Cs. You have to build around content connectivity, and not just a place, price, or product because the marketplace changes so rapidly. All of this is that marketing changes, so we have to change, too. We can't be addicted to comfort.

With the four Cs, I believe they're all equally as important. If I had to lean toward one, it would probably be campaigns. The reason is that the other Cs are part of the campaign, so it's the overarching delivery mechanism. But content is where you have to start, a connection is how you get there, and the conversion is what makes it happen to be successful. But the campaign is the delivery of all of these, so make sure your campaign is the overarching ability to deliver.

I have a vision of where marketing should go. Friction should be removed from the consumer experience, and preferences should be saved or curated by businesses, so you shouldn't have to tell them that you like your hotel room at 67 degrees. It should just be there when you arrive. When you choose to buy something, you should look at your phone with your face and say, "Buy," and it buys it. Distractive and intrusive marketing should disappear. I think marketing should go away from commercials that interrupt, and interruptive marketing should disappear because the consumer knows what they want now. We've come a long way, and as a society, have become more sophisticated when it comes to advertising. We figure out what our wants and likes are, and we almost don't have to be told or convinced through the rhetoric of marketing. The good marketing will find you before you even have to figure out you need it.

Marketing is way more important than just promoting or selling something. I think marketing can be a movement of ideas. It can be a changing of communication. But it's why, when governments are taken over, one of the first things that is controlled is the communications process. In battles, you try to take down your opponent's communication facilities so they can't communicate. The press is often taken over or edited/censored by governments when regime change happens because that's how they market their ideas to the public. So, marketing is more than just selling something. Marketing is delivering ideas, movements, execution of those ideas—and it can change the world.

Marketing is ultimately vulnerability because you're putting a message out there, and when you put anything out, there's feedback. A lot of folks are scared of marketing, of the vulnerability of putting themselves out there, so not everyone's a great marketer. You may be great at making music, you may be in a band that creates beautiful music, but if you can't find a way to market it, no one will hear it. And then you can't move on with your trade to make yourself happy. You may make beautiful paintings, but someone has to market that for you to get it into the public space to recognize you and so that you can create a living.

Vulnerability can be a good thing because it makes us adjust to our weaknesses. And I'd say sometimes self-doubt is selfish because you've been given talents, but if you doubt your abilities, you might not be able to deliver that talent to the world. As a marketer, your talents are delivered through marketing and often through successful brand messaging and through the delivery of a message. Not everyone can be a great marketer, but I think if you stick to the fundamentals and learn from them, you can still find success in delivering your message, as well as what you want to do with your marketing career.

I believe marketing can be learned. I don't know if anyone is born a great marketer, but there are certain traits. Extroverts are good with people marketing; introverts are good with creative marketing. Malcolm Gladwell wrote that 10,000 hours or more of experience in any subject will make someone an expert, or at least very good at it so practice your marketing crafts such as copywriting, etc. as much as possible.

If you want to be a copywriter and have a message, write all the time. Learn how to write copy and headlines that attract people. If you want to be a cinematographer, make a lot of video. Learn how to edit over and over again, then throw it away and then edit over and over again because you don't come out of the womb ready to do any of this stuff. There are technical things to learn—lighting, sound, audio—and then there are innate things that you'll have, such as creativity. Repetition in marketing makes a better marketer, which in turn makes a better professional.

This book is meant to be a foundational resource for marketers and people that want to successful brand marketers. We touched on many specifics, tactics, and ways to deliver marketing. Also, there are tons of lessons available online today. At no time in human history has it been this easy to connect, to get information out, and to receive information, whether it be through Facebook, CRMs, social media, or buying copywriting and other marketing services. There are also many masterclasses online and in-person that I encourage you to go learn about on your own time. This book is also meant to be an introduction and help you understand and implement the four Cs. Use this as the seed to help you grow as a marketer because, if you happen to miss your chance, there's *no more next time.*

ACKNOWLEDGMENTS

Writing a book is challenging. No matter how good (or bad) the finished product is, the time and effort is painful. I don't envy people who make their living writing because doing it as a side hustle is enough to know I don't have the patience. Podcasting is so much easier. So, in case I never go through the painful process of book writing again, I need to thank and point out a few people.

Let's start with Emily, the wife. She holds down our house with three busy kiddos and a lot of animals, six at print time, so I can chase my marketing dreams and nightmares. I love you and appreciate how we've been a team, in good times and bad, trying to navigate each other's messes and the big world outside. Thanks for being there for our family and especially for me. You're the best.

To Maggie: 1.2.3. SFC, huh! To Bert: May the Force be with You. To Banks: Let's snuggle and watch a movie. Y'all make me want to be a better dad every day.

A big thank you to Renasant Bank and my work family. What a special place to earn both my job and living every single day. I'm especially thankful for Robin McGraw, Mitch Waycaster, Kevin Chapman, Scott Cochran, Rocky Miskelly and Jim Gray. In addition, a special thank you to my marketing team because as our team theme goes, *we don't keep the pace, we set it*. A third thanks for Jamey Logan, Ashley Gambrel and Emily Wright for editing a "few" pages of this book on the first run through.

I have to thank my partner in marketing crime and the Marketing Money Podcast, Josh Mabus. Just about everything in this book was a discussion at some point between us. The good ideas in here are probably all his, and, as I tell him when he has one, which is quite often, "consider it stolen." LMFG.

Another thank you to Mabus Agency for helping Renasant, our marketing, and me look good. A special thanks to Corey Childers, who works his tail off for us and also designed the cover of this book.

Thank you to the American Bankers Association who have supported me through providing a platform to teach marketing, share my marketing war stories, and hopefully pass on a little knowledge to America's bankers.

Thanks to these people who need to be thanked for being a mentor or providing counsel at various points in my career, many of whom have no idea they did: Jack Reed, Jr, George Taylor, Glenn McCullough, BB Hosch, Kate Young, Bob Kish, Brad Middleton, Guy Mitchell, Mike Armour, Carter Baker, Chris Rogers, Danny Dinkler, Suzanne Smith, Amy Tate, Geoffrey Yoste, Gordon Fellows, Grant Fox, James Waters, Eric Pelletier, Debbie Brangenberg, Kim Hutchens, Mr. Mike, Louis Holmes, John Robinson, Morgan Baldwin, Ed Broyhill, Bob Strickland, Chris Neeley, Roy Coffee, Richard Burr, Jim Tobias, Becky Mathis, Nancy Streblow, Mr. Howell, Dr. Mike McCready, Raymond Cass Patrick, Reed Hillen, Robert Hall, Wallace McMillian, Ken Cyree, David Rumbarger, David Brevard, Duncan Ham, Wood Chatham and many others that slipped my mind when I typed this.

Finally, thank you to my parents, Cliff and Sharon, grand-parents, Papa and Granda, and in-laws, Bob and Jane Black, for supporting our family and me. And to my brother, Clayton, and sister, Sarah, and your families; I hope you have many, many accolades. Know that all of you are loved and appreciated.

A "P.S." thank you to Kristen White and her team for helping me to finally get this book over the finish line. Whew, that's all for now.

ABOUT THE AUTHOR

John Oxford didn't choose marketing, it chose him. At age seventeen, Oxford found his first job as a taste-tester and commercial viewer for Nabisco. Taste-testing snacks and watching commercials may seem like a sweet gig, but a young man can only eat so many Nutter Butters and Oreos. Oxford decided to put his professional career in the ad world on hold, opting for college instead.

Fast forward to today. Oxford now uses his well-honed skills in brand messaging as Director of Marketing with Renasant Corporation—the parent of Renasant Bank—with assets at print time of approximately $13.4 billion, 2,500 employees, and more than 200 locations in the United States.

In addition, Oxford is the marketing section instructor at the Graduate School for Banking at LSU, an instructor at the American Bankers Association's Stonier Graduate School of Banking, and a former co-chair of the American Bankers Association's Marketing Conference Board.

Prior to joining Renasant, Oxford served in the administration of President George W. Bush as a legislative assistant to the Executive Office of the President with OMB.

Oxford was named Top 40 under 40 in Mississippi in 2007 by the Mississippi Business Journal.

He and his wife make their home in Tupelo, Mississippi, with their three very active children, a dog, four cats, a tortoise, and whatever else needs a home.

EDUCATION

Certified Financial Marketing Professional Designation —
Institute of Certified Bankers at Northwestern University
M.A. in Government — Johns Hopkins University
B.A. in Communication and minor in Political Science —
University of Tennessee

CONTACTS

Text: 662-205-6288
Email: campaignmarketinghelp@gmail.com
www.johnoxford.com
www.marketingmoneypodcast.com

ON SOCIAL MEDIA

linkedin.com/in/john-oxford-38607a4
facebook.com/john.oxford
twitter.com/johnoxford1